JOHN
Fred B. Craddock

KNOX PREACHING GUIDES
John H. Hayes, Editor

John Knox Press
ATLANTA

Library of Congress in Publication Data

Craddock, Fred B.
  John.
  (Knox preaching guides)
  Bibliography: p.
  1. Bible. N.T. John—Commetaries.
2. Bible. N.T. John—Homiletical use. I. Title.
II. Series.
BS2615.3.C7 1983   226'.507   82-48095
ISBN 0-8042-3236-9

© copyright John Knox Press 1982
10 9 8 7 6 5 4 3 2
Printed in the United States of America
John Knox Press
Atlanta, Georgia 30365

Contents

JOHN

Introduction

Introducing the Gospel of John to the Preacher

If any book can be at the same time both familiar and unknown, then the Gospel of John is that book. To say that this Gospel is familiar is to say that the church has remembered fondly and almost easily many of its lines and scenes. Many readers have preferred Jesus' open declaration of who he is (the Christ, 4:26; the Son of God, 5:17–18; the Son of Man, 9:37) in this Gospel over the veiled statements of the secretive Jesus of the Synoptics. And apparently uninhibited by the profundity of John's language, the church has embraced effortlessly the rich images by which Jesus' ministry is interpreted: bread, water, life, light, vine, way, door, shepherd, and many others. No less familiar are some of the vivid scenes sketched by this Gospel alone: Jesus at a wedding in Cana, Jesus and Nicodemus, Jesus and the Samaritan woman, the raising of Lazarus, Jesus and his mother at Golgotha, and the questioning of Simon Peter, "Do you love me?" Even the casual churchgoer has learned John 3:16 in Sunday School, has been comforted by "Let not your hearts be troubled" (14:1) at funerals, and has heard hope in "I am the resurrection and the life" (11:25) at Easter.

Even so, this Gospel remains in many ways a mystery, not only to laity but to clergy and to scholars as well. Early in the third century the brilliant Origen began writing a

commentary on John and his notes on chapters 1-13 exceed-
ed 32 books. And to this day the flow of volumes about this
Gospel continues, addressing the many unresolved questions.
For example, there is as yet no consensus as to who wrote
this book, to whom, when, where, and why. Although the
church has traditionally associated this Gospel with John the
son of Zebedee and affixed his name to the title, this apostle
appears by name nowhere in the text. Instead there are re-
curring references to "the other disciple" or "the disciple
Jesus loved" (13:23; 18:15–16; 19:26; 20:2–8; 21:7, 20–24).
Some scholars who do not accept these as self-references do
see them as possibly the venerating expressions of a Christian community that claimed a line of tradition and hence
authority from one of Jesus' close associates (21:24). Tradition has also located the origin of this Gospel in Ephesus, but
this tradition, too, suffers from a lack of solid evidence.
Equally uncertain is any clear assignment of date. Older
studies, based on an evolutionary scheme, were inclined to
see in this "spiritual" Gospel with its "advanced" Christology a product of late first or early second century Christianity.
More recent studies have tended to argue that an earlier date
is possible though by no means certain.

The student of the Gospel of John does seem, however, to
walk out into the clear light of certainty when addressing the
question of purpose, for the book itself provides a statement
on that subject. "Now Jesus did many other signs in the presence of his disciples, which are not written in this book; but
these are written that you may believe that Jesus is the
Christ, the Son of God, and that believing you may have life
in his name" (20:30–31). Here is an apparently clear announcement of an evangelistic purpose, with the equally
clear implication that the book was intended for unbelievers.
But what unbelievers? The Gospel is certainly aware of a
strong and attractive sect of John the Baptist, but the author's way of dealing with them carries more the mood of
polemic than of persuasion (1:6–8, 15, 19–42; 3:25–30;
5:33–36). And the language used for portraying "the Jews"
would hardly empty the synagogues and fill the churches
(1:17; 2:13–22; 3:10–15; 8:39–47, and many others). Others
have understood "that you may believe" to be addressed to
Christians who are not in possession of the full, liberating

truth which the writer's witness seeks to supply. For example, the placing of Simon Peter in a role secondary to the disciple Jesus loved (13:23–25; 18:15–18; 20:2–9; 21:7–23) could be taken as referring to a Petrine circle of believers who were Christians but who were not abiding in the full light. It could be the case, however, that the book was written for Christians whose faith was being battered by hatred from the world (17:14) and expulsion from synagogues (16:2). These believers may have been experiencing, in addition, the deadly erosion of distance in time and place from the originating events (20:29). Faith must be continually generated in those who believe as well as those who do not. Whoever the addressees were, the text makes it abundantly clear that the message is from believers to believers. Notice, for example, the inclusive "we" in faith statements throughout the book (1:14–16; 3:11; 4:22; 21:24). And quite clearly the instructions, the promises and the comfort of the farewell discourses (chaps 14–16) are to and for the community of faith.

It may be said, then, with some confidence that the Gospel of John was written and read in a church with problems within and without. A new generation of believers seeks assurance that the word they received is indeed in continuity with Jesus and that it is no less effective for succeeding generations who have not seen and yet believe. Apparently their needs are such as to call for what, in the writer's opinion, is the definitive presentation of Jesus and of the word to be entrusted to the community of faith.

That John's portrait of Jesus is radically different from that of the other Gospels is apparent to even a casual reader. The absence of much material common to the Synoptics, the presence of much unknown to them, and the rearranging and remarkably different telling of those accounts held in common make the question of John's relation to the Synoptic traditions exceedingly difficult. Fortunately, preaching from this book does not wait upon the solution to this and countless other problems that continue to surround this extraordinary Gospel in which "a child can wade and an elephant swim."

Introducing the Preacher to the Gospel of John

The preacher should be pleased to discover that the writer of the Gospel of John is a fellow preacher. This is not to say

that this Gospel is solely a source for sermons but is itself an
example of Christian preaching. It is no mystery why the
Gospels (and much of the Old Testament as well) are easier
to preach than the epistles. Gospel materials were shaped by
oral transmission and hence came to us already possessing
sermonic quality while epistles began as script and hence do
not move as easily into oral form.

What precisely does it mean to call the Gospel of John
preaching? It means first of all that the writer of the Gospel
is very conscious of the distance between the readers and the
originating events in the ministry of Jesus and seeks in many
ways to negotiate that distance. Every preacher who has
stood between an ancient text and a congregation awaiting a
word knows the unavoidable difficulty of that distance. In
fact, the whole task of interpretation is finding for one group
of persons the meaning of a text which was written with
other persons in mind. We sometimes forget that even
though the distances of time and place and circumstance between the Gospel writer's situation and that of Jesus and the
Twelve were not as great as we experience, still they existed
and, if left unbridged, could become productive of error and
destructive of faith. And so the writer goes to work after the
manner of every preacher. There is language distance and so
he translates: Rabbi means Teacher; Messiah means Christ;
Cephas means Peter, etc. (1:35–42). There is geographical
distance and so he explains: "Now there is in Jerusalem by
the Sheep Gate a pool, in Hebrew called Bethzatha, which
has five porticoes (5:2); "Jesus went to the other side of the
Sea of Galilee, which is the Sea of Tiberias" (6:1). Matters of
culture and custom foreign to the reader demanded clarifica-
tion: "For Jews have no dealings with Samaritans" (4:9).
And, of course, there is the problem of time. John's readers
needed to know that passing time had not destroyed the authority of continuity with Jesus himself ("He who saw it has
borne witness—his testimony is true and he knows that he
tells the truth—that you also may believe," 19:35); that those
so removed had no less access to saving faith ("Blessed are
those who have not seen and yet believe," 20:29); and that
the Christ who returned to glory had not abandoned the
church on earth ("I will not leave you desolate; I will come to
you," 14:18).

Efforts by preachers to negotiate distance generally follow one of two patterns. One pattern consists of a simple twofold presentation: first, the historical sketch of what is done or said in the text, and then the application to the reader or hearer. Much "biblical" preaching follows this outline. The other pattern is to retell the story of the past so that it speaks directly to the reader or hearer. This is the method of a Gospel, and especially the Gospel of John. The writer seeks to say who Jesus is in and for the community addressed.

To refer to the Gospel of John as preaching is also to say that certain central themes pervade and inform the entire narrative. Even though it is the nature of a Gospel to be constructed of units of materials which may have circulated earlier as distinct and separate pieces of tradition, in their present form these units serve a larger purpose with governing theological perspectives about God, the world and human life. This is not to say that the preacher will want to force unity and harmony upon materials that exhibit some divergences of thought, but it is to say that preaching from any one passage in John should be nourished and disciplined by the principal emphases of the whole book. For example, one could hardly preach from this Gospel and not give attention to eternal life, knowing God, the truth, abiding in Christ, the word, believing, and the Spirit.

And finally, the Gospel of John is preaching in that the writer employs certain communicative techniques, certain literary devices by which the message is presented to the reader. There is, for example, the regular pattern of a sign and then a sermon, a sensory act followed by a discussion of the truth to which that act witnessed. A technique unique to John among the Gospels is the use of words with double meanings: there is bread and then there is bread; there is water and then there is water; there is the temple and then there is the temple; and on and on. Such a device puts the listener-reader in a crisis of decision, being judged by what is seen or heard. When the writer says that the Word became *flesh* and *we* beheld his *glory*, the clear implication is that not all saw the glory; some saw only the flesh. The preaching of this Gospel therefore conceals as well as reveals; some see and some do not. In this connection, the writer uses the misunderstanding of those about Jesus who see but do not perceive as the occasion for discourses on the truth that has been missed. Another method of communicating common to the Gospel of John is the private conversation which is gradually enlarged into a sermon to everyone. Jesus and Nathanael, Jesus and Nicodemus, Jesus and the Samaritan woman: these and other conversations move out of private into public discourse so that it becomes clear that Jesus is not addressing one but all. In sum, the writer is a skilled communicator who obviously realizes that the word resides not just in the events of the story but also in the telling of the story.

Before turning to the text itself with suggestions for preaching the text unit by unit, a few general guidelines might be useful.

One, read and become familiar with the whole Gospel before preaching a single sermon from it. The whole will enrich and discipline each message; anticipation can be generated for subsequent sermons in the series; the entire series of sermons will strike the listener with their unity rather than each message standing in isolation; and like the Gospel itself, the messages will have upon the listener a cumulative effect.

Two, stay within the Gospel of John for the sermons rather than reading a text from John and blurring it consciously or unconsciously with material from the Synoptics when they carry accounts of the same or similar events. For example, the healing of the blind in John 9 is not to be confused with the healing of the blind man in Mark 8. Let John say what John has to say.

Three, beware of the seduction of quotable quotes and apparently simple images, as though repeating them is enough to communicate meaning to modern listeners. This is a very strong temptation when preaching from John whose analogies of light, water, bread, door, shepherd, way, vine, and word seem to carry an immediacy of meaning without need of a commentary. In fact, these terms caress warmly the listener's mind, but they convey little concrete meaning, let alone the writer's meaning, without interpretation. The preacher's unavoidable task is to listen to the text and then preach what is heard rather than repeating the words as though that alone made preaching "biblical."

Four, be careful not to transfer automatically the battles in which this Gospel engages to the present context of one's hearers. Some struggles of those early Christians do, of course, continue even now, but that is a judgment to be made in each case. However, to bring uncritically the writer's polemics into the present can be a sham battle and perhaps even an exercise to avoid today's real issues. For example, this Gospel's elevation of the beloved disciple above Simon Peter has been used by Protestant pulpits to attack the Roman Catholic Church in which the primacy of Peter is maintained. Or again, the Johannine community's bitter struggle with the Jewish synagogue can and has provided Christian sermons the texts for generating and encouraging anti-Judaism. The writer sought to say who Jesus is and what Jesus says to the Gospel's first readers; the preacher will be true to the text who does the same for his or her listeners.

Finally, the preacher will want to avoid arrogance in the use of this Gospel. The warning is appropriate when using any text, but to the unwary, John especially seems to launch sermons into a mood of superiority. The reason is that the writer is letting the readers in on the true meaning of things, sharing insights missed by the original audiences of Jesus. *We* have beheld his glory, says the author, and that conclusion is shared with persons who accept it without wrestling with the offense of the incarnation: whoever has seen Jesus has seen God. The modern preacher, from a comfortable distance and armed with a faith that has the benefit of Easter and centuries of hindsight, must be on guard against reading these texts with condescension. "Stupid Nicodemus! Shallow Samaritan woman! Blind disciples! Obstinate Jews!" Always the distinction is to be made between the reader's experience of the text and the experience of persons who appear in the text. After all, Jesus' contemporaries did not have the Prologue to the Gospel of John to tell them who the Nazarene *really* was.

THE PROLOGUE
TO THE GOSPEL
(JOHN 1:1–18)

Probably every preacher has, from time to time, been drawn to the Prologue of the Gospel of John as a text not only deserving, but demanding a sermon. All the qualities one could ask of a text are here: truth that is timeless, ideas which stretch mind and imagination, affirmations that are lifegiving, significance for every human being, and a central theme which gives the passage unity and completeness of thought. And yet these very qualities send many scurrying away in search of another, for preachers want to master the sermon text, to wrap the mind and emotions around it in order to share it with confidence. This text resists such mastery, towering above all the homilies which have attempted to reveal its heights. Some of those who have not backed away overwhelmed later confessed to dissatisfaction with their vague lectures on the pre-existent Word or inadequate explanations of Christology. So often sermons on the Prologue are doctrinal essays, efforts to demonstrate who Christ *really* was. But even when not clear, these messages are generally well received because they offer a very high Christology. And after all, who could object to a minister bragging on Jesus? Other preachers have felt the only way to handle the wealth of this treasure is to offer it to the congregation in small portions. There is a wisdom in that and in the comments that follow the reader may find evidence to support a decision to preach a series of sermons on John 1:1–18.

Even so, let the preacher entertain the possibility of a single sermon on the whole passage. Texts do not always have to be mastered. There is immense value in taking the hand of the congregation and leading it up close to a huge passage where it can stand with face upturned in awe and wonder. What so many sermons lack is not truth or clarity or relevance, but size. With this in mind, how shall this grand text be heard and spoken?

It may be well to observe at the outset that this text is experiential; that is to say, the writer savors again in the telling the recent meeting with God through the person of Jesus Christ. According to this Gospel the fundamental human longing is for God. This has been true from the moment Adam stirred in the moist clay until our present straining to see beyond the heights to catch one glimpse of ultimate reality. In fact, to know God is life eternal (17:3). But since no one has ever seen God (1:18), Philip speaks for all of us when he says to Jesus, "Lord, show us the Father and we shall be satisfied" (14:8). It is, therefore, to all of us that Jesus replies, "He who has seen me has seen the Father" (14:9), or as the Prologue expresses it, "the only Son, who is in the bosom of the Father, he has made him known" (1:18). To call this text experiential, then, is to be reminded that it is not a doctrinal statement in which an understanding of God is used to explain who Jesus Christ is. Rather, the experience of Jesus was for the Johannine church an experience of God.

This fact leads naturally to the second observation: John 1:1-18 is *confessional* in nature. This quality is signaled by the introduction of "we" and "us" into the text: "dwelt among us": "We have beheld his glory": "from his fulness have we all received, grace upon grace." With these words the Christian community accepts the fact that what it has seen and heard has not been the common experience of the general public. That Jesus of Nazareth revealed God was not obvious to all and sundry. The Word became *flesh*, and that is all many could see, but with faith's eyes "we have beheld his glory." The Word of God upon the ear is a whisper and not all hear it. As this Gospel will say later, God answered Jesus' prayer, but some said it thundered (12:28-29). As we will notice throughout the Gospel, the signs and speeches of Jesus are followed by doubt and faith, confusion and understanding. Whoever would confess faith must have the courage to do so amid questioning, disagreement, rejection, or even ridicule. Faith does not wait for a majority vote.

In the text before us, the form of the confessional is *poetic*. To say a passage is poetic is not to say it is less serious but rather that it is evocative, suggestive, stirring up meanings in the reader rather than defining. Poetry is especially appropriate when the topic is God and the purpose is confession, for we do not have here a subject that will sit for a photograph nor submit to precise description. The burden of definition is upon the writer; the burden of poetry is shared with the reader. And, of course, even poetry is here inadequate but it is hardly surpassed when expressing the inexpressible.

John 1:1–18 consists of three stanzas with prose inserts about John the Baptist at vv. 6–8 and 15. When one wishes to preach a series of sermons on the Prologue, each stanza could well serve as a text. Vv. 1–5 relate God and all creation through the Word; vv. 9–13 relate God and all human life through the Word; vv. 14–18 declare God's offer of grace and truth through the Word become flesh, Jesus Christ. This passage is not unique in making such sweeping affirmations about the Word. Commentaries on this Gospel will provide ample background materials and analogies in Jewish literature proclaiming the creative, sustaining, redeeming work of the Word or its feminine parallel, Wisdom (see, for example, Prov 8, Sirach 24, Job 28). More will be said below about the theological significance of the Word.

A fourth characteristic of the language of the Prologue is that it is *polemical*. In addition to the Christian community introduced by the expression "We have beheld his glory," these verses make the reader aware of two other communities of faith: the followers of John the Baptist (vv. 6–8, 15) and the Jewish synagogue ("For the law was given through Moses," v. 17). The writer acknowledges that both John the Baptist and the Mosaic law are from God, but at the same time insists that there is in Jesus Christ not only a unique revelation of the unseen God but an offer of grace and truth. Such is the character of this Gospel's polemic: not an emotional denial of any Divine source for the other faiths, but neither an easy embrace of everything under the guise of generous ecumenism. The preacher of John's Gospel has to come to terms not simply with the relevance of this text but with the claims of truth it boldly makes. Otherwise, one's sermons will be undercut with apologies for this early Christian writer. No one preaching in this or any other century can do so ignoring the fact that the Gospel is presented in a marketplace of religions and philosophies making claims upon the hearers. Everything is at stake here: ethical values, human and natural resources, social and political relationships and fullness of personal life. No one is served by a shallow embrace of every "faith" from materialism to yoga, as though serving tea to all proclaimers makes one more human or more Christian. The Fourth Evangelist was very aware of the groups across the street when he stood up to preach. While one may be uncomfortable with some of his comments about the Jews and the Baptist movement, in one respect he instructs us all: it makes a difference what you believe.

Finally, the language of the Prologue is *theological*, laying the foundation upon which the entire Gospel is constructed. And here the word "theological" is intended specifically since the subject is God, a fact sometimes overlooked when studying New Testament texts. Some preachers would give you the impression that God is the subject of the Old Testament while Christ and the Holy Spirit are the subjects of the New. However, careful reading of the texts themselves persuades otherwise.

God is portrayed here as both distant from and related to the world. That God creates, provides, reveals, and redeems *through the Word* implies a distance between God and creation, a distance that is positive. In a time of rapt attention on personal relationships, the notion of distance has been denied proper value. However, without distance even relationships that are marked by love and respect can become diseased with loss of individuality and freedom, one person being consumed or at least becoming a satellite to the other. The text tells us that God is God regardless of how we feel or whether we relate as creatures. God cannot be captured within our subjectivity nor granted existence by our "good vibes." God cannot even be known except by revelation. This proclamation that "God is" sits in quiet judgment of a generation narcissistically preoccupied with itself.

But distance is not the only word; God also gives light and life, empowers us to become sons and daughters and comes to us in the flesh. This language is quite intimate: those who believe are *born* of God (v. 13); the Word has pitched its tent among us (v. 14); or a bit later, "God so loved the world"

(3:16). As the classic formulations have expressed it, God, not
being identified with the world, *can* help us; God, being identified with the world, *will* help us.

As for the Christian's view of "the world" the starting
point according to John 1:1–18, is that through the Word,
God creates, sustains, redeems it. And this means all the
world. The language is so strong as to appear polemical: *All
things* have been created through him and *not one thing* without him. Why so forceful? Some ancient religions looked upon the world as having another source, being the work of a
lesser god or an evil god from whom the good god delivers us.
The evidence of such deliverance was total disengagement
from the world in all its manifestations. The human body,
the natural order, all social and political structures were to
be negated because from these the soul sought to be set free.
While no Christian pulpit proclaims two creators, one of evil
and one of good, some do in fact give that impression with
their preachments of a kind of private salvation that tolerates no responsible engagement with one's social context nor
encourages any care of the earth. To be sure, we will encounter passages in this Gospel which set the life of faith over
against "the world," but in every case, the interpretation
must not counter the affirmation of 1:1–18. Of course, the
writer is realistic enough to know there is evil, darkness, and
death in the world, but these are due to human choice and
not to anything in the nature of the world. Some have loved
darkness rather than light (3:19); some choose to live by appearance rather than by the truth (7:24). As we will notice
repeatedly, worldliness in this Gospel is not a term referring
to bad habits, questionable forms of pleasure, nor to the ac-
quisition of material possessions. Sermons warning of these
erosive forces must find texts elsewhere. For this Evangelist,
worldliness is exhibited in the structure, tradition, customs
and administration of religion so entrenched as to resist the
judging and liberating Word which threatens vested interests. It might be well to warn ourselves in advance that all
texts which confront worldliness will be speaking of Scripture, clergy, holy days, sacred duties and revered tradition.
These passages remain no less incisive today in all places
where the church has uncritically embraced the economic
and political values which guard self-interest. At this point

perhaps we need only to remind ourselves that we cannot, in the name of God the creator or of Christ the agent of creation, embrace the human or natural world as though it were something more than created; neither can we ignore or reject the human or natural world as though it were something less than created of God.

And, says John 1:1–18, we have come to understand this because of God's revelation in flesh. No higher compliment could come to the human community than that the Word had joined it, in flesh. We do not come to know God through dream, or prophetic ecstasy, or sudden rending of the veil of clay. "The Word became flesh"; that is to say, the Word came in a particular time and place, subject to all the conditions of human life; a person among persons, Jesus of Nazareth in Galilee. This means, of course, that the revelation being veiled in flesh is not obvious, especially to those who insist that all manifestations of God have been encounters of another kind, in another place, to another person. To mention Jesus of Nazareth is to say, then, not only that God is revealed but that God is concealed. Jesus of Nazareth? God whispered and those waiting for a shout heard nothing. Those who heard and saw did so by trust, without guarantee. To those who will not, final proof is never enough; to those who will, final proof is not necessary. "We have beheld his glory," says the writer, and that insight of faith will provide the lens through which the story of Jesus will be projected upon the reader's mind.

(Nothing has been said here about the two parenthetical comments concerning John the Baptist. Vv. 6–8 and 15 will be incorporated into the witness of John beginning at 1:19.)

JESUS' MINISTRY AS A REVELATION OF GOD
(JOHN 1:19—12:50)

The Witness of John the Baptist
(John 1:19–51)

V. 19 offers a title for the material that begins the Gospel narrative: "This is the testimony of John." In common with all the Gospels, this writer undertakes the tedious task of giving adequate but not too much coverage to John the Baptist whose movement was alive and well and in a real sense a competitor of the church. Each Gospel affirms that John is a messenger of God, a voice in the wilderness calling the people to preparation for the Lord's coming, fulfilling Isaiah's prophecy (Isa 40:3). Mark even calls John's ministry "The beginning of the Gospel" (1:1). But the Christian communities saw John's ministry as meaningful only in relation to Jesus and therefore pointed to that subordination in a variety of ways. Matthew, for example, speaks of John's reservation about baptizing Jesus, preferring that Jesus baptize him (3:13–15). Luke creates the same effect by referring to John's imprisonment before describing Jesus' baptism, in which account no mention is made of the one who baptized Jesus (3:19–22). In the text before us, Jesus' baptism is omitted altogether, thereby removing any special status that act may have given John, as well as preserving the status of Jesus as the eternal Son from the presence of God.

The Testimony of John Himself (1:19–34)

The witness of John falls naturally into two parts: his witness about himself (vv. 19–28) and his witness about Christ (vv. 29–34). John's witness concerning himself, like the parenthetical references in the Prologue (vv. 6–8, 15), is couched in the language of debate: "He confessed, he did not deny, but confessed" that he was not the Christ. That the investigating team consisted of priests and Levites implies that a central concern was not only John's identity but the rite of baptism. John refuses to make any claim for himself either as Messiah or as forerunner of the Messiah; he is a witnessing voice. Nor does he make any claim for his baptism as a proselytizing act or as effecting forgiveness or as related to the Holy Spirit. In other words, says the writer, John's baptism had nothing of the purpose or efficacy of Christian baptism. John's baptism is in water and functions in his overall ministry of helping to reveal the Son to Israel (v. 31).

The preacher of this text will probably wish to comment on two significant facets of this brief narrative: First, there is the clear implication that the church, in dealing with the person and role of John, was faced with the fact of strength, capacity, and effectiveness. A weak or even mediocre prophet would not have been effective, but neither would he have been a problem. The church has trouble knowing what to do with persons of capacity and power. Usually a good job is done of picking up cripples and attending to the weak, but many ministers are afraid or intimidated by persons of wealth and power. Instead of addressing the Gospel to these who also need its judgment and promise, clergy and lay leaders often seem satisfied if such persons sponsor Christian projects here and there. It is no less true that strong and effective ministers find themselves competing in the affection and loyalty of their parishioners with the Christ to whom they are supposed to witness. Temptation is always commensurate with ability; the greater the ability the greater one's temptation. We would probably be better on guard against errors of pride and misuse of our gifts if we gave more attention to strength rather than to weakness. Vulnerability is at the point of capacity.

A second reflection upon John 1:19–28 could focus upon the examination of John by the "Jews from Jerusalem." It is customary to applaud prophets and ministers who arise outside the establishment with no credentials except the word of God. Such is the habit of our culture: the private eye is the hero while the police force is portrayed as bungling and ineffective. And there is no question but that God does call persons from the outside to address the word to those inside. We recall not only the Old Testament prophets such as Amos, but John the Baptist and even Jesus. But we need also to recall that we celebrate the work of these without credentials from a safe distance long after history and Scripture have certified them as messengers of God. Why not look to our own time and to the multitude who claim to speak for God today and test the spirits to see if those who "are not of us" are of God? Whatever we may conclude in retrospect about the canons of judgment and the results of the investigation into John's ministry, the fact remains that there was and is something commendable about the effort to check the truth claims of John's message. To be a leader among the people of God is to protect the flock from quacks, fakes, frauds, and false prophets. Distinguishing between the apparent and the real is most difficult and anyone who attempts it may exercise poor judgment and stand over against a person or movement which is truly of God. But even that error is to be preferred to the failure to make any effort at all to alert the flock to the existence of hirelings and false shepherds.

The second part of John's witness (vv. 29–34) is to Jesus Christ as Son of God and as "the Lamb of God who takes away the sin of the world." One must be careful not to let Synoptic material bleed into the story. There is no account of Jesus' baptism, no splitting of the heavens, no voice from heaven. Only the descent of the Spirit is mentioned and John witnesses it (unlike Mark 1:10–11 in which Jesus is the recipient of these signs) in order that he might know Jesus is the Son of God and the one baptizing with the Holy Spirit.

Two phrases are extremely important in this passage and in the theology of the entire Gospel. The first is John's twice stated admission, "I myself did not know him" (vv. 31, 33). Couple this with John's earlier word to the Jews, "among you stands one whom you do not know" (v. 26) and the sum of it is, neither the synagogue nor the Baptist sect really understood who Jesus was. But this is more than a polemic; the New Testament as a whole concurs with this text that no one knows who Jesus is except by revelation. Knowing the Son is by God's revelation (Matt 11:27); flesh and blood has not made him known (Matt 16:17); no one can say Jesus is Lord except by the Holy Spirit (1 Cor 12:3). The foundation for all

Christian proclamation, therefore, is capsuled in this narrative about John: revelation and witness. To abandon these in
favor of some logical or historical "proofs" is to remove the
possibility of faith in favor of some more controlled and managed response to Jesus.

The second key phrase in 1:29–34 refers to the Holy Spirit descending and *abiding* on Jesus (v. 33). Jesus is the permanent bearer of the Spirit. We will have many occasions to
notice this Evangelist's use of *abide* or *stay* or *remain* to describe that relationship between Jesus and God and between
Jesus and his disciples which is deep and sustained, a relationship marked by knowledge and life. Here it is enough to
keep in mind that the Spirit is given to Jesus and it is Jesus
who gives the Spirit to his followers (20:22). In the farewell
speeches the writer will repeat insistingly that the Holy Spirit is no alternative to Jesus. On the contrary, the Holy Spirit
is from Jesus, reminds of Jesus, testifies to Jesus, reveals
Jesus, has no ministry apart from Jesus. Why is this important to say? In both the first century and the twentieth, some
have claimed in the name of the Holy Spirit styles of spirituality that avoid the demands of discipleship laid down by
Jesus. The Fourth Gospel tolerates none of this: there is no
Christian spirituality that does not listen to and obey Jesus of
Nazareth.

As to John's reference to Jesus as the Lamb of God, the
preacher will want to be cautious. The Old Testament allu-
sion is rich: the passover lamb, the sin offering lamb, the
warrior lamb of the apocalypse. The problem lies in discerning the writer's meaning. In what sense, according to John,
does Jesus take away the sins of the world? The commentaries will discuss the alternatives, but indecisively because the
writer's intention is unclear. True, Jesus lays down his life
for the sheep (10:11) but actually the death of Jesus is hardly
developed as an atonement such as one meets in Paul and
elsewhere. In John's crucifixion account, Jesus dies as a
lamb, not as a sin-removing sacrifice but as the passover
lamb (19:31–37). All this is to say that honest caution in handling 1:29 demands that the preacher not play too imagina-
tively upon the figure of the Lamb of God. One can, of course,
explore for the listeners the various possibilities and their
implications for the Christian's experience of Christ, but un-

certainty as to the writer's intended meaning must not be
withheld from them. The church has the right to share in
what is unknown as well as what is known. Perhaps it would
be wise to refrain from a sermon on this Christological title
at this point, in favor of a sermon later at 19:31–37 where
Jesus is presented as the passover lamb, whose death ends
one kind of passover and initiates another.

The Testimony of John's Disciples (1:35–42)

So dominant has been the impact of the Synoptics that
their sequence of John's imprisonment, Jesus going to Galilee to begin his ministry, and the call of the first disciples
will intrude itself here unless resisted. In this Gospel, John
and Jesus have parallel ministries in Judea, and Jesus' first
disciples come to him from John's following. The shift of disciples from John to Jesus dramatizes the writer's understanding of John's relation to Jesus. More striking, however,
is the way in which this Evangelist provides the reader with
a model of how witnessing to Christ functions. John witnesses to Jesus and points two of his followers to Jesus. These
two come to Jesus and learn firsthand by "abiding" with
Jesus the truth of the word they heard from John. Then one
of the two, Andrew, goes to his brother and witnesses to him,
inviting him to experience the Christ for himself. Thus
through the testimony of believers the circle of faith widens.
Understood in this manner, conversation that otherwise
seems awkward takes on significance. Note the movement of
the language of witnessing:

> What do you seek?
> Where are you staying (abiding)?
> Come and see (used again at v. 46).
> They stayed (abode) with him that day.
> We have found the Messiah.

They heard, they sought, they experienced, they witnessed.

In fact, says the writer, this is the way Simon Peter came
to be a disciple of Jesus; his brother Andrew shared the word.
At the time of the writing of this Gospel, Simon Peter is well-
known, so much so that even though it is Andrew who introduced Simon to Jesus, it is Simon who introduces Andrew to
the reader; he is Simon Peter's brother. But the process of

believing began with Simon in the same way it begins for all:
by hearing the word spoken. Even though the preacher of
this text may want to focus here on the little-known Andrew
whose claim to fame is that he "passed it on," it would be
well to mark for later use this first in a series of treatments of
Simon Peter. For reasons not altogether clear, Simon is not
portrayed as pre-eminent among the disciples. On the contrary, his understanding, information, and insight about
Jesus come to him from others. Simon is a recipient, not a
dispenser (13:23–25; 18:15–16; 20:2–10; 21:7–8).

It might be important for the preacher to ponder the
meaning of one other phenomenon in 1:35–42: the appearance of Aramaic words which are translated into Greek. Why
are "rabbi," "messiah," and "Cephas" used and then explained? One immediately assumes that the readers are
Greek–speaking and unfamiliar with Aramaic, but if so, why
not just use Greek in the first place? After all, Simon is called
Peter in v. 40 before the word is explained in v. 42 as a translation of Cephas. Have these words become so imbedded in
the tradition that by this time they are formulaic and even
sacred? Maybe. What is significant here, whatever the mo-
tive at work, is that the strange and distant sounds of Aram-
ic are not dropped, dismissed, replaced by the language of
the reader; rather, they are preserved and translated. To
have preserved them without the translation would have
been to practice magic: the old religious words, though
meaningless, still work. To have lost the words, leaving the
readers with *only* a translation would have been to cut off the
readers from the past, giving them a message dislodged in
time, orphaned without mother or father. The writer's handling of these three words is reminiscent of his handling of
the person of Christ: neither locked in the past by a rigid his-
toricism nor set adrift in the present without reference, like
an ink blot test, meaning anything and everything and therefore nothing.

The Testimony of Friends of John's Disciples (1:43–51)

In this paragraph, the circle of believers in Jesus widens
even further, having begun in Judea and now spreading to
Galilee, having begun with the lone figure of John the Baptist

and reaching through John's disciples to their friends. In
fact, as we shall see below, in v. 51 the circle widens to include the readers of this Gospel.

In order not only to understand but also to enjoy this
story, one needs to recall the perspective announced in the
Prologue: the Word became *flesh;* we have beheld his *glory.*
This is to say that the accounts of Jesus' work and words
have been and can be encountered on two levels: one, the level of the apparent, that which is available to any public eye
and ear; two, the level of revelation, the glory (presence of
God) available to the eye and ear of faith. While witnessing
to what the Christian community has seen and heard in
Jesus, the writer still carries in the narrative the other perspective as well. The preacher would do well, in sharing
these Johannine accounts, to keep both perspectives active
and available. After all, for faith to be a possibility, doubt has
to be a possibility and not a continually discredited,
cartooned possibility. Faith sickens and dies in a room where
doubt is laughed at.

The story, then, comes to us at first in a plain, straight-
forward way. The scene is Bethsaida (contra Capernaum in
Mark 1:21, 29), the witness is Philip, and the listener is Nathanael. The word to Nathanael is a word of faith, that Jesus,
son of Joseph of Nazareth, is the promised Messiah. The response is a reasonable one: the credentials of Jesus hardly
qualify him as the one described by Moses and the Prophets
as the people's deliverer. Those among us who regularly evaluate strangers by place of origin, residence, family, educa-
tion and station should not find Nathanael's response out of
order. Upon the invitation to join in faith's inquiry ("Come
and see"), Nathanael meets Jesus' supernatural knowledge
and is persuaded.

At this point the story assumes more of the qualities of
level two. Nathanael's confession of faith is too enormous,
too elaborate, to have been prompted by Jesus' special
knowledge. It seems now to be the case that Nathanael is
voicing the community's faith, not just what a person would
say upon meeting Jesus. In fact, as the "true Israelite," Nathanael, who is never mentioned in the lists of Jesus' disciples in the other Gospels and Acts, could be the paradigm of
believing Israel, those Jews who accepted Jesus as Messiah.

Such a view is further supported by the identification of
Jesus with Jacob (whose name became Israel) at Bethel (Gen
28:12). Angels descending and ascending as at Bethel dramatically identify Jesus as the very place, the house of God's
presence. In him heaven and earth are joined; he is the "gate
of heaven." That a simple story of meeting Jesus is elaborat-
ed into a Christian proclamation is even more clearly evidenced by the shift to the plural form of "you" in the
dominical saying in v. 51: "Truly, truly, I say to *you*." That
which began as private conversation is now obviously sermonic: Jesus speaks to all the hearers (readers). The obser-
vant preacher will surely find in this form of movement
(from conversation to proclamation) a pattern of communication that is not only quite effective but one that is also congenial to the nature of a Gospel that does not pound the
listener into a choiceless corner.

A final comment about this passage: vv. 50–51 reveal a
quality in this Gospel that will manifest itself repeatedly, a
quality so positive and helpful that it should appear often in
sermons from this book. No Gospel reveals the writer's
awareness of the reader so often and so clearly as does John,
and the mood of that awareness is invariably encouraging
and supportive. At the point in a narrative in which the focus
is enlarged to include the readers in Jesus' audience (as here
in vv. 50–51), a favorite phrase of this Evangelist is "greater
things than these" you will see or do. This is a clear and
strong word to Christians who live at a distance in time and
space from the ministry of Jesus of Nazareth. Such Christians as this Gospel addresses could very well feel themselves
to be second class believers, those who get their faith from
the script and not from the central characters themselves.
"Back then they had Jesus and the Apostles; today we have
words on paper." The writer is very sensitive to the discour-
agement and sense of loss which could and probably did in-
fect and disease the church. To that condition the writer
speaks repeatedly: not everyone present at Jesus' ministry really perceived; much of what Jesus said and did even the disciples understood only after the resurrection; the revealing
word in signs and discourses is active and effective at all
times and places; subsequent generations of disciples will
see, hear and do greater things than these; blessed are those

who have not seen and yet who believe. This is one message in John which rather than diminishing in relevance with the passing of time actually increases. From our distance, such a Gospel is *really* Good News.

The Witness of Jesus' Itinerant Ministry
(John 2:1–4:54)

In Galilee—The Wedding at Cana (2:1–12)

The first sign (2:11) and the second sign (4:54), both performed at Cana of Galilee, mark off a cycle of stories that are difficult to characterize by any integrating factor. To speak of them as stories of Jesus' itinerancy is not really helpful since geographical notations by this writer do not seem consistently significant. Perhaps, as some scholars have suggested, designating the signs by number may be a clue that the writer is using a source that consisted of a list with descriptions of signs Jesus did. One must be tentative in the face of slight evidence. Whatever may have been the original intent of such tags as "first" and "second," they can serve us practically as convenient limits that allow us to examine a manageable unit of material. As for the geographical references, it may be enough at this point to notice that Galilee, held in low esteem in official circles of Judaism, was generally hospitable to Jesus while Jerusalem and Judea were centers of suspicion, rejection, and death.

The preacher should consider using 2:1–12 and 2:13–25 for sermons in tandem. The two stories have much in common and the listener will be aided in having this pointed out without, however, having to hear it repeated with each message. Since Johannine stories have very similar formats one must beware lest the listeners have their ears dulled by repetition. Both the wedding story and the temple cleansing story are revelation events (manifest the glory of the Son); both are third day stories (resurrection symbolism); both focus upon a sign; both carry a polemic against religion centering upon ceremonies (water of purification in one, temple rites in the other); in neither does being present suffice to generate faith in Jesus; both conclude with references to disciples believing. But the differences between the two and the wealth of meaning in each justify two messages, not one. In Galilee is the wedding; in Judea is the funeral ("Destroy this temple").

The first sign in Cana makes two very important points about the life-giving revelation of God in Jesus Christ. The first is the non-contingent nature of that which God does in Christ. The rather sharp remark of Jesus to his mother (2:4), to be repeated to his brothers (7:3–10) and shown in his relation to good friends (11:1–6), serves to sever all words and deeds of Jesus from the suggestions, pleas, or demands of anyone, whether family, friends, disciples, or enemies. Jesus acts and speaks from above, from God, according to his "hour." This characterization of Jesus' ministry is disconcerting because it removes his actions from the realm of compassion and general response to human need. This is not to say that this Evangelist regarded Jesus as cold and lacking in sympathy. It is rather to say something else about what God is doing in Jesus Christ. Strange as it may seem at first, we are in this description of Jesus' ministry being totally from above encountering a strong doctrine of grace. All the benefits of Jesus' words and actions are *given*, independent of anyone's claim upon him. "From his fulness have we all received, grace upon grace" (1:16). Translated this means that the initiative is with God and not with us, that earth responds to heaven, not heaven to earth. As Nicodemus will be told later, life in the kingdom is from above and no one brings it down by calculation, effort, special claim of place or character, not even Jesus' mother. Harsh as Jesus' word to her may seem to some, it was an encouraging word to the church receiving this Gospel, wondering whether the second and third generation Christians living in another country were being denied the blessings that seemingly were reserved for the few in the original circle. Not so. This doctrine of grace says that time, place, proximity, and even family ties do not dictate the self-giving of God. We do not set up the conditions for God's self-disclosure. Let those who prefer compassion to grace ponder this for awhile. Stories of Jesus' compassion are movingly beautiful and prompt Christians to act likewise in their own circles of influence, with compassion to those nearby in need. Grace, however, reaches to all persons at all times. Compassion provides more wine to avoid a social disaster; grace provides a manifestation of God, and to know God is life eternal.

The second significant point about the epiphany of the Son at Cana is that the message is revealed/concealed. Such is the meaning of calling an act a sign: some get the point, some *ooh* and *aah*, others scratch their heads and confer, while other see absolutely nothing at all. Were one to draw concentric circles around the sign of Jesus revealing his glory (that is, Jesus acting so as to reveal a truth about God), the innermost would represent the disciples; they believed in him (2:11). Interestingly, the ones already committed to Jesus and who are following him are those who see beyond the wine and believe. For this writer, seeing, knowing, understanding and believing are joined to commitment and obedience, not to intelligence and proofs. Believers are those who live within understanding distance of God. "If any man's will is to do his will, he shall know whether the teaching is from God . . ." (7:17). In the next circle would be the mother of Jesus who believes her son has the power to act so as to rescue the occasion. As Nathanael believed in Jesus as having special knowledge, so does the mother of Jesus believe he has special power. But no more is said; her concern is the wedding of a friend or relative and only in that arena, only at that level, does she expect Jesus to act. In the same mood, Martha and Mary will expect Jesus to act to save the life of their ill brother, Jesus' friend (11:3, 21–22). But in both stories Jesus does not do what is expected by those who make request but rather what he chooses. And what he chooses is to make God known so as to make abundant life available to all who believe. In the third and outermost circle would be the steward of the feast, smacking his lips, savoring the good wine, and congratulating the host. He is totally of the earth, oblivious to the whence and whither of life in his small world of tastes and smells.

The preacher should not go beyond the text to satisfy the curiosity of those who refuse to hear the message but who insist upon satisfaction concerning matters of fact lying back of the text. The Fourth Evangelist would say that the word to be heard is *in* the text and curiosity about possibilities of historical verification is an exercise in unbelief. To set the line of arguments and proofs whereby one can believe is intellec-

tual works righteousness. In fact, Johannine theology would
say that there would be no saving value were such a process
to eventuate in believing Jesus did in fact perform such a
miracle at Cana. This Gospel is full of accounts of those who
believe he worked the signs but who did not believe in him as
the revealing Son of God. On the other hand, a blessing is
granted those who have not seen and yet who believe (20:29).
As significant as signs are in this Gospel, they are not simply
presented as miracle stories to be investigated. Perhaps this
is why details are so lacking. As signs these acts of Jesus are
to function as windows rather than ornaments. Seekers after
miracles usually need *one more* to be fully persuaded, all the
while missing the signs along the way.

In Jerusalem—Cleansing the Temple (2:13–25)

This story is important for all four Gospels, but this Gospel highlights its theological significance by removing it
from logical and chronological considerations. It is reasonable to assume that the Synoptics have the better location for
the story if one is following the gathering opposition to Jesus
and the developing web of circumstances that precipitate his
arrest and death. Cleansing the temple, they say, is the last
straw. This Evangelist, by excerpting it from such a context
and setting the account strangely and dramatically at the beginning of Jesus' ministry, is able to focus entirely upon the
event itself and the fundamental issues at stake. By removing
it from any historical frame, the writer says to the reader,
"Listen to what is really taking place here."

The temple cleansing is a passover story; that is to say, it
is a story focusing upon Jesus' death and resurrection. The
feeding of the multitudes which prompts a sermon on Jesus'
body and blood is a passover story (Chap. 6), as is the account of Jesus' death as the passover lamb (19:31–37). And
when discussing Jesus' death and resurrection, the Fourth
Evangelist is not concerned with *causes* of his death, as
though cleansing the temple or any other act *caused* his passion. His death was not caused by anyone or anything in this
Gospel. He died when "his hour" came; then he laid down
his life and he took it up again (10:17–18). In fact, even here
Jesus says to the Jews, "Destroy this temple" and the verb is
imperative. He commands the events of his life because the

work and words of Jesus Christ are from above and are not responses to historical circumstances and human contingencies. As with his life, so with his death and resurrection: they are from heaven.

And what is the significance of Jesus' passion in the context of this passage? He replaces the temple of wood and stone with himself. He had revealed the divine glory by replacing water of ritual purification with the wine of the Messiah. He had cleansed the Jewish temple and called it "my Father's house." But now in response to a request for a sign he gives the ultimate and final sign: by his death and resurrection Jesus would end religion that sought to meet God through observances of places, times, rituals, customs, and other managed arrangements. The hour has come when worship of God is not according to place but according to God's own nature as spirit (4:21–24). If temple means the meeting of God and human seekers, then Jesus is the temple, he is Bethel, he is the house of God. As is customary in this Gospel, Jesus' auditors hear and see by appearance not by truth, standing confused while admiring the building which cost 46 years of labor. That marvelous edifice, intended as a witness to God, had been distorted into an object of religious devotion. Now an obstacle rather than an aid, the temple is ripe for destruction.

But the crucial question is, Why is the writer saying all this to the church of his day? Why talk about something of another time and place that no longer exists? Was the church to get an ego boost and dance triumphantly over the grave of a collapsed system of religion? If we are not careful, preaching the Johannine texts can nourish such hollow arrogance and even anti-Judaism. One can only conclude that within the church being addressed there existed the clear danger of drifting or being enticed into the very same error again. With the passing of time, the Christians tended to replace old customs, traditions, rituals, and institutions with new ones. Not that these are intrinsically evil; of course not. Rites and places are not just permitted, they are essential. But within them the ancient evil lurks. Some will absolutize the rite and the place and lose sight of the One to whom they are to witness. Replace the old church building and some members quit attending; replace the minister and some members drop

out; change the order of worship only slightly and the dis-
gruntled exit noisily. "Destroy this temple and in three days I
will raise it up." And some will respond, " It has taken forty-
six years to build this temple." Must Christ then be crucified
again, and again, and again?

In Jerusalem—Conversation with Nicodemus (3:1–21)

The Nicodemus story is almost a case in point, particu-
larizing the general statement about belief born of signs in
2:23–25. This transition summary in 2:23–25 provides an opportunity for the preacher to offer the congregation an alternative to the conversionist language that pervades the
churches. It is common to describe the spiritual state of listeners to the Gospel in either/or, belief/unbelief, saved/lost
categories that are the legacy of revivalism. Without negat-
ing the appropriateness of that vocabulary for some situations ("Choose you this day. . ."), a sermon on 2:23–25 could
provide another and for some a more realistic understanding
of one's relationship to Christ. In this and many other texts
the reader encounters different qualities or levels of faith. In
Jerusalem there was a kind of faith generated by Jesus' signs,
but the fact that Jesus did not trust such believers testifies to
the inadequacy or incompleteness of such faith. Apparently
these believers had not seen beyond the signs to Jesus as re-
vealer of God. We have already noticed that faith in Jesus'
special power (Jesus' mother at Cana) and faith in his supernatural knowledge (Nathanael) are qualitatively different
from that faith in him as the epiphany of divine glory. As we
shall see in subsequent stories, the ideal faith is that characterized as "abiding" in Christ. But the point here is that
many shades, depths, and qualities of faith are found in those
who surround Jesus. In the course of following Jesus, an act
or speech by him could offend some and move them farther
away or deepen faith and move some into stronger discipleship. For example, in 6:66, many of the disciples are offended
by the eucharistic message describing Jesus as the bread
from heaven and they turn back. Or again, in 20:24–29, the
last "convert" made is not only a disciple but one of the
Twelve. According to this Gospel, one does not decide for or
against Jesus Christ once and only once. In each new situa-

tion, before each issue, in every relationship, that decision of faith is made anew. Even disciples must become disciples again and again. This presentation of the life of faith as alive, capable of growth or regression, more nearly corresponds to the experience of many of us than does the image of a once-in-a-lifetime decision, responding to the word of Jesus as a melon responds to a knife.

The story of Jesus and Nicodemus demonstrates the writer's point; there is faith, there is faith, and there is faith. Nicodemus comes in a kind of faith that is unclear and uncertain, apparently seeking to get sufficient evidence to move that faith into clarity and certainty. Rather than providing that nourishing and persuading proof, Jesus demands a radically different perspective on the Kingdom of God.

The preacher would do well to attempt to do no more than follow 3:1–15 and to let the sermon unfold in the same manner as the text. The writer here provides a model of one format for effective preaching. First, the scene is set: two men meet in private "at night" (the form of the Greek word designates *kind* of time, not a point in time or duration of time). The reader is thereby alerted to a conversation shrouded in mystery. Second, the conversation begins in a manner predictable between two teachers with a common interest. Third, through the use of the common Johannine device of double meanings, the reader sees emerging two widely divergent views of life in the Kingdom. A word which can be understood in two ways is used by Jesus to speak of birth "from above" and is heard by Nicodemus as being born "again." Nicodemus is confused. (It is striking that in the current popularity of this text, Nicodemus' understanding—born again—is preferred over Jesus'—born from above.) Fourth, the private conversation becomes a sermon at v. 7: "You (plural) must be born from above." The plural *you* clearly signifies that the word of Jesus is being addressed to many. The fifth and final stage in the unfolding story is the enlargement of the conversation to a debate between the church, represented in the person of Jesus, and the synagogue, represented in the person of Nicodemus. That we have here a post-Easter Christian sermon is evident in several ways: Christian baptism and its association with the Holy Spirit has already been mentioned in v. 7; the pronouns be-

come *you* plural (vv. 7, 11, 12) and *we*, that is, you Jews and
we Christians; and the ascension of Christ is referred to as a
past event (v. 13). In addition, the story has to be post-Easter
because the Spirit was not yet given, says the writer, until
after the ascension (7:39). Were the narration understood
solely as an event from the earthly ministry of Jesus, then
Nicodemus would have been commanded to do what was not
even a possibility until after the resurrection and ascension
of Christ.

Here, then, is an excellent way to preach. A conversation
between two persons gradually opens into a debate between
two perspectives represented by those two conversants and
institutionalized in the church and the synagogue. And what
is the issue? What is at stake? No less than life in the Kingdom of God. One orientation, said to be "of the earth," seeks
to line up sufficient proofs and arguments so as to arrive at a
clear conclusion and thus believe or not believe. According to
this perspective, faith is thus to be born and sustained, having carefully moved through historical and logical evidence
and arrived at its conclusion without risk, cost, vulnerability
or decision. The other orientation insists that life in the Kingdom is given of God, from above, unearned, and unachieved.
Being from above, the life eternal is uncontrolled, uncharted,
and uncalculated. It is as mysterious as the whence and
whither of the wind.

What we have in John 3:1–15 is a message on the radical
grace of God, written to a community that must have been
tempted to make the church into an egocentric program of
Kingdom building, or perhaps to return to the synagogue
with its secure and guaranteeing traditions, structures, rituals, writings, doctrines, and moral instructions. The writer
allows that church to overhear Jesus tell a synagogue leader
that the life abundant and eternal is *from above* and as such
leaves those wanting to succeed in religion bereft of speeches, claims, explanations and plans for achieving. New life is a
gift; one believes or one does not. Paul nowhere presents the
word of grace more radically than does the writer here. It is
regrettable that so many sermons on grace give the impression that grace is the law made easy, or that God has lowered
the passing grade, or that the time of permissiveness has
come. No such moral distortions of grace can be found here.

The text's strong assertion of God's initiative defines clearly the listener's role: to trust and to receive.

A sermon can treat 3:16–21 quite independent of vv. 1–15. Nothing in vv. 16–21 is reminiscent of the conversation with Nicodemus nor dependent upon it for clarity. In addition to the Prologue, this Gospel contains a number of these theological summaries or overviews which gather up the central messages of the book under such controlling concepts as life/death, light/darkness, truth/falsehood. Nor does the meaning of this paragraph depend upon a decision as to whether vv. 16–21 contains the words of Jesus or are the writer's own. In the Gospel of John, attempts at red-letter editions of the New Testament fail completely.

The reader will detect immediately that 3:16–21 is a theological reflection upon the meaning of Christ's coming into the world and as such, is similar to 1:1–18, 3:31–36 and a number of other passages. The preacher who lays out a series of sermons from this Gospel will want to plan carefully in advance to avoid repetition as well as neglect. Most of these theological summaries have a governing image or germinal idea that helps cast new light on ancient truth. Here the controlling image is light. John 3:16 is a statement about God's act of love for the world, the sending of the light which reveals God. To use John 3:16 to refer to the cross would not be Johannine since, for this writer, the saving act is the coming of the Son to reveal the God whom none have seen. The cross is only one phase of the grand drama of the Savior's sojourn from God to God.

The central thrust of 3:16–21 lies in its startling realism and honesty. While sending a light into a dark place is motivated by love and a desire to help, not all are helped. Some hate the light and its painful revelations of the way they are: their priorities, their prejudices, their hates, their deceit. For these the light is not a blessing but a judgment. Turning on a light in a room full of rats and roaches is not an occasion of joy for rats and roaches. But the analogy can help us understand how a single act, bringing light into a room, can be both blessing and judgment. This, says the writer, is the crisis created by the coming of a knowledge of God as Creator, Sustainer and Redeemer. All of us have known persons who can enter a room with no thought of being critical or judgmental and yet whose presence alters conversation and conduct, creating in some a general sense of discomfort and guilt. The entire Bible is very much aware of the negative side of a good and benevolent act. A stepping stone can be for some a stumbling block; a feast can be for some a cause of illness and distress. As the Gospel of Luke expressed it, "Behold, this child is set for the fall and rising of many in Israel, and for a sign that is spoken against . . . that thoughts out of many hearts may be revealed" (2:34–35). The Christ child appears: some rise, some fall; the saving presence is for some a disturbing presence.

This fact, faced squarely by biblical texts, is very difficult for some to accept as descriptive not only for the role of Christ but of the church and the ministry as well. Some prefer to think that only good flows from a well-intentioned act or word, but it is only in fairy tale worlds that turning on a light produces no shadows. Any church or minister that would be a decisive center and force for truth and human good must live with the crises created by truth and goodness. It is in the very nature of every act that turning toward one in helpfulness is turning the back on another. Suppose a doctor enters a room full of very sick people. Turning to help one is turning away from another. The only alternative is to stand there in a pool of pity and feel sorry for them all equally.

God did not send the Son into the world to judge the world but the coming of the Son is unavoidably the judgment of the world. "And this is the judgment, that the light has come into the world and men loved darkness rather than light" (3:19). Or as this Gospel's Christ was to say later in a farewell speech, "If I had not come and spoken to them, they would not have sin; but now they have no excuse for their sin" (15:22). It is a sobering thought for the church and the minister to ponder: Do we really want to make a *difference;* that is, to be the agent of crisis?

In Judea—The Final Witness of John the Baptist (3:22–36)

In this section John the Baptist (or more appropriately, John the Witness) is introduced and dismissed a final time. The texture of the material is noticeably different from the preceding verses just as the introduction of John at 1:19–42 differed from the theological discourse in 1:1–18. An almost puzzling concern for historical details of time, place, and activity (vv. 22–24) provide the transition into the "John testifies that Jesus is greater" paragraph (vv. 25–30). As in 1:19–42, the issue in dispute is the interpretation of John's baptism and the result is the same: John points from himself to Jesus and John is pleased that his disciples shift loyalty to Jesus. The only noticeably new item here is the change of image from that of servant being unworthy to untie the master's sandal thongs to that of an attendant of the bridegroom being happy that all attention and favor are accorded the groom. The attendant has no other reason for being. The repetition of this very similar material reminds us how strong was the presence of the Baptist's followers in or near the Johannine church and how important it was for the writer to protect the Christian flock from such an attractive but erroneous competitor. Unless one is faced with a situation analogous to that of the writer, wisdom would advise against repeating so soon the sermon generated by 1:19–42.

Having dismissed for the last time the Baptist, the author extols the Son as the only one from above and hence the only one who can testify directly concerning God and who can speak the truth. The Son is from the Father, possesses without limitation the Spirit from the Father, and therefore is the very presence of the Father on earth. One's relation to the Son is in effect one's relation to the Father. This has been said before in this Gospel and will be said again. However, the closing verse of the paragraph states most forcefully a theological perspective of this Gospel that deserves attention in more than one message: eternal life is a present reality. "He who believes in the Son *has* eternal life" (v. 36).

This emphasis on eternal life as a present rather than a future state of being is not confined to 3:36; it was expressed in 3:18 and will appear again in 5:24, 10:28, 11:25, 17:3 and numerous other places. But given the conditioning of many Christians to think of eternal life as descriptive primarily if not solely of the realm beyond the grave, it would be well to begin now to let the message of this Evangelist enlarge the congregation's perspective on eternal life and enrich its life of faith.

When the writer defines eternal life as knowing God

through trust in Jesus Christ (17:3), it is established at the
outset that eternal life is a qualitative and not a quantitative
term. "When we've been dead ten thousand years. . . . We've
yet more days to sing God's praise than when we first begun"
may be a poet's way of translating "everlasting" but it does
not translate "eternal life." Traditional and popular approaches to the term "eternal" presuppose that the question
is, How long does it last? More appropriate is the question,
What is the nature of such life? According to the Fourth
Evangelist, eternal life is life which trusts that what Jesus
Christ reveals about God is true. And what is revealed? That
the world is not for us an alien, hostile, and evil place but
rather is the creation of God who gives to it and to us light
and life; that God loves the world and comes to it in order to
make possible a relationship described as being empowered
to be children of God; that this relationship is one marked by
grace and freedom; that worship and service are the appropriate responses to God's initiative; and that this relationship is a continuous and growing one, best described as
"abiding" in God.

It follows, then, from such understanding that the abun-
dance of such a life does not wait until after the grave in order to be known and experienced. "He who believes in the
Son *has* eternal life" (3:36). There is nothing transforming
about morgues and funeral parlors; the transformation
comes at the point of faith in Jesus Christ. It is he who makes
the difference; eternal life begins there or it does not begin.
In fact, so radically does the Gospel assert this truth that it
continues with the declaration that unbelief is a state of
death, a state of living under judgment (3:18), under the
wrath of God (3:36). According to this perspective, one does
not think of living and then dying, perhaps to live again but
rather of being dead and then, upon faith in Christ, passing
out of death into life (5:24), never to die again.

To preach such a message would, of course, raise questions about the future beyond the grave and about resurrection. Such questions one would anticipate and, if not
forthcoming, should be generated by the preacher. One
would be well advised, however, not to try to include both
present and future understandings of eternal life in one sermon. Trying to give both sides equal time in one message

may sound fair and democratic but such procedure, in fact, weakens the truth of each side. Every sermon ends in a tie. Only one emphasis can be made on any one occasion; to underscore too much is to underscore too little. A good sermon is heretical in that it does not attempt to say everything that is true. Save, then, for another text and another time the message about eternal life as future. The Fourth Gospel will provide such a text, for just as tomorrow does not consume today, neither does Johannine theology allow today to consume tomorrow.

In Samaria—The Conversation at the Well (4:1–42)

The story before us contains so many pregnant lines which could serve as sermon texts (vv. 13–14, 23, 35, 38 and others) that the preacher must guard against mutilating the narrative beyond recognition. The story is so beautifully unfolded with all the Johannine touches which we are beginning to recognize that one would do well first to preach the main line of the narrative, then the subordinate story, and then, if desired, two or three minor but important themes.

The principal story is that of Jesus, the woman and the Samaritans. It would be appropriate for a message on this text to be itself in narrative form. The movements within the story are basically two. First, there is the geographical movement of the Gospel, quite reminiscent of Acts 1:8: from Jerusalem, to Judea, to Samaria, to the world. In John 4, Jesus moves from Jerusalem into Judea and then into Samaria. The story closes with the affirmation, "We know that this is indeed the Savior of the world" (v. 42). In fact, John 4 achieves in brief what is achieved in Acts 1–8 which records the gradual spread of the Gospel from Jerusalem and the Jews to those "afar off." Whether or not the similarity between John 4 and Acts 1–8 justifies a theory of kinship or dependence can be traced through the commentaries. However, one's conclusion about such speculation has no real bearing on the thrust of the text here. For the writer to say that Jesus "*had* to pass through Samaria" (v. 4) is clearly not a statement about historical or geographical necessity. Jesus' obligation to pass through Samaria is a theological statement, consistent with "for God so loved the world." By the time this Gospel was written the Samaritan mission of Philip, Peter, and John (Acts 8:5–25) had already occurred. Whatever may have been the attitude of the Jerusalem church toward Samaritan Christians, the Johannine church clearly affirms the strength and quality of the faith of these despised people.

The second and more extensively developed movement in the main narrative is that of a growing and deepening faith. If the geographical movement is outward, the faith movement is toward the center; that is, from the outer edges of unbelief as the conversation began to a closing confession of faith in Jesus Christ as Savior of the world. The story opens with the beginning of a conversation which has in it no promise of anything fruitful. The conversants are not only distanced from each other as Jew and Samaritan, as man and woman in a public place, as strangers, but in typically Johannine fashion, their worlds are so far apart that they use the same words with quite different meanings. What she means by "water" and what Jesus means by "water" are poles apart (recall this "double talk" about the temple in chap. 2 and the new birth in chap. 3). Soon, however, the distance is narrowed by the woman's curiosity about this man who puts himself in the category with, or rather superior to, Jacob, whose well it was and about whom many stories were told. For example, when Jacob lifted the cover from the well, bubbling (living) water rose to the surface. Next, curiosity gives way to recognition of Jesus as a prophet (v. 19) because he tells her all about herself. Here is a faith in Jesus based upon his having supernatural knowledge, quite similar to that of Nathanael who believed because Jesus knew him before they met (1:47–49). But in the Johannine church, unlike some modern Christian communities, believing Jesus has supernatural power or supernatural knowledge is not sufficient faith. Faith is not bragging on Jesus nor using complimentary adjectives; the faith toward which the writer moves the reader is faith that "beholds the glory," that comes to know God through Jesus.

The faith of the Samaritan woman continues its pilgrimage. Having begun in talk with a stranger, it moves through curiosity to acknowledging Jesus as a prophet. The way now has become painful for the prophet Jesus has forced her to look at herself. The old and still prevalent strategy of evasion is used: start an argument. "We Samaritans think our church is right and you Jews think yours is right." The maneuver fails as the woman is drawn out beyond all her defenses and hears herself express a hope she probably had not verbalized in years. "I know the Messiah is coming." "I am he" (vv. 25–26).

Sadly, the woman's faith pilgrimage seems to stop here. There is no evidence she was convinced Jesus was the Christ. She witnessed to others with the question, "Can this be the Christ?" (v. 29). Her repeated affirmation, beyond which she seemed unable to move was that here was a man "who told me all that I ever did" (vv. 29, 39). One has the clear sense in this Gospel, however, that had she confessed Jesus to be the Christ, this would not have been adequate. For this Evangelist, Jesus is the Christ, but more than the Christ. Jesus is not fully confessed when called the fulfillment of Jewish messianic hopes; he more than fulfills human expectation. Jesus is not simply God's Messiah; he is God's presence among them. In fact, any single title by which one confesses faith in Jesus is insufficient and reductionistic.

The faith pilgrimage recorded here has its conclusion, then, not in the woman but in the Samaritans of the village. This is evidenced in two clear ways: Jesus "abode" with them two days (abiding is the heart of faith), and their confession acknowledges Jesus not simply as expected Messiah, but as Savior of the world (v. 42). As such, he embraces and is embraced by Jewish believers, Samaritan believers, all believers.

Before moving attention away from the woman, two minor themes may be worthy of development in preaching this story. One is the writer's portrait of this woman as of the earth, or of the world, or "from below" as Johannine language puts it. Just as the wine steward enjoyed the wine and missed *the* wine; just as the Jews centered upon the temple and missed *the* temple; just as Nicodemus struggled with understanding physical birth and missed the birth from above, so the woman's life is trapped in a non-satisfying, non-fulfilling cycle of filling and emptying water jars, marrying, divorcing, and re-marrying. Whether life's little rituals be religious or secular, at the altar or at the town well, they are no substitute for knowing God.

The other minor theme worthy of consideration is that of the woman as witness. Her own faith apparently stopped short of that full insight and trust extolled by the writer, but she witnessed to the full extent of her faith. In fact, she invited others to affirm what she herself only entertained: "Can this be the Christ?" It is impressive that her witness initiated a relationship between others and Jesus, the fruit of which was a faith beyond her own. We would be well advised that witnessing need not wait upon having full faith in full measure. And we would be well reminded that the work of the Word of God is such that it can generate in listeners a faith that exceeds that of the speaker. The efficacy of the Word is not totally contingent upon the faith of the one speaking the Word. The gospel conveyed by a sparrow may produce an eagle.

Within the larger story of 4:1–42 lies a subordinate account involving Jesus and the disciples. This section (vv. 31–38) is a self-contained unit and may be treated as such without fear of distortion by isolation from the context. The disciples have been removed from the principal story by reason of their having gone into the village to buy food (v. 8). We may reasonably take the conversation of Jesus with the disciples as the vehicle for presenting the word of Christ directly to the church. Interestingly, such direct conversations between Jesus and his immediate followers are rare in this Gospel prior to the farewell sections beginning in chapter 13. The idea that the church is directly addressed by the risen Lord in chapters 13–21 but only indirectly overhears messages from the preresurrection Jesus to his followers in chapters 1–12 is a division that often breaks down. The Fourth Evangelist does not distinguish between the word of the historical Jesus and that of the risen Lord now addressing the church. The paragraph before us is a case in point.

By going into Samaria Jesus leads his disciples in a mission to Gentiles. Their response is not all commendable. They leave Jesus to go for food; they do not understand his talking with a woman, much less a Samaritan; they are silent rather than witnessing; they continue to think of food for the body when Jesus speaks of that food which is doing God's will (vv. 32–33). It is not really of primary importance whether the "others" who preceded these disciples in the Samaritan mission (v. 38) refer to the prophets, to John the Baptist and his followers, or to early Christian missionaries as described in Acts 8. The point is, taking the Gospel to the Gentiles has the authorization of Jesus himself, the time for that mission is now because the harvest is ready, and the followers of Jesus are immobilized by misunderstanding, prejudice, and distorted values. The barriers of race, class, and economics remain to this day, and the record of the church in overcoming them has not markedly improved. Granted, the movement of the Gospel from its Jewish birthplace to the Gentiles was a crisis of immense proportions, receiving attention from every major New Testament writer. But to extend the word of God's favor beyond the borders of Israel was not exactly a radically new departure without antecedent in the Hebrew Scriptures. In Abraham all the families of the earth were to be blessed (Gen 12:3); all nations would flow into the Lord's house on the highest mountain (Isa 2:2); God's Spirit was to be poured out upon all flesh (Joel 2:28–32); and the books of Ruth and Jonah testified to the universal reach of God's grace. One would think that a little Bible reading would have prepared the disciples for witnessing in Samaria. But it did not, and it does not. To know what the Scriptures teach, and to embrace that teaching as demand and promise are two very different experiences, and between them lies the familiar story of confusion, misunderstanding, and resistance. Not even the authorization of the mission by the word and precedent of Jesus has noticeably improved the performance of the church in the Samarias of the world.

Return to Galilee—The Healing at Cana (4:43–54)

With this account the cycle of stories that began with the first sign in Cana now concludes with Jesus again in Cana. The format is familiar; a general introductory comment (vv. 43-45) followed by the encounter between Jesus and the official, just as in 2:23–25 there was a general statement about Jesus' reception in Jerusalem, followed by the story of Jesus and Nicodemus (3:1–15). However, in the introduction to this Cana story there is one unusual line: Jesus enters Galilee because a prophet has no honor in his own country (4:44). In the Synoptics, this proverb is quoted upon Jesus' rejection in his own home *in* Galilee (Matt 13:57; Mark 6:4; Luke 4: 24).

The text before us implies that Jesus' own country was Judea (Jesus the true Judean?) or perhaps even Samaria (8:48). It is unclear whether the fourth Evangelist intends to correct the Synoptics or whether he is simply reflecting a different tradition. Whatever may be intended, one should not make too much of a Judean rejection and a Galilean reception. Already this Gospel has recorded rejection and reception in both places.

The healing of the son of the official from Capernaum (vv. 46-54) is called a sign by the writer and therefore is to be understood as a revelation story; it is recorded to open some truth to the reader. That characteristic of miracle stories in this Gospel accounts for the noticeable absence of descriptions of Jesus' compassion or of the crowd's response, elements familiar to us from Synoptic miracle accounts. However, John 4:46–54 has enough similarities with the accounts in Matt 8:5–13 and Luke 7:1–10 of Jesus healing a centurion's servant in Capernaum that the preacher must beware lest those texts bleed into the text before us, producing a sermon from a combination of the three rather than from John 4:46–54. Of course, one will want to pay attention to commentaries which discuss these similarities and differences in pursuit of the larger question of the relation between the Synoptics and the Gospel of John. However, such analyses should serve the preacher by putting into sharper focus the distinct qualities of the present text so that it may be heard and spoken. The sermon itself ought not be burdened by comparative studies to the point of confusing the listeners.

One will notice upon reading 4:46–54 how the story form is quite like the earlier Cana sign (2:1–11). There is a need expressed; Jesus resists; faith in his power persists; Jesus deals with the problem in a way different from the expectations of the one seeking help; servants function in the interchange; faith results; but in each case believers are those who already believed (disciples in the one case, the official in the other). But beyond the similarities in form lies a striking statement in this story that probably is its center: "The man believed the word that Jesus spoke to him. . ." (v. 50). Here is faith in the word alone, without the embroidery of ritual, without the scaffolding of signs and wonders, without proofs, evidences, and guarantees. The relation between faith and signs is variously portrayed in this Gospel. At times signs seem to generate a kind of faith and at others, faith seems an essential prerequisite to seeing that a sign has been given. However, in the case before us the word of Jesus is heard and believed. The official has penetrated to the heart of the matter—the word. To believe the word is to know who Jesus is, the word in flesh.

In presenting the story of the word of Jesus effecting a healing and of a man's belief in that word, the writer is not just offering the reader a model of strong faith or correct faith. Here the Evangelist is underscoring the word as powerful and effective and faith in that word as sufficient faith. The readers, removed by time and place from the earthly ministry of Jesus, have no reason to feel cheated, distant from the scenes and opportunities of the "golden age," forced to live on the recorded memories of how great it was when Jesus was here working wonders. The word is not confined to the bodily presence of Jesus. In this story, it was spoken in *Cana* and a person was healed in *Capernaum*. The Johannine church has that same word and therefore has access to the power of God. Because of the presence of the word in the church, ours is not a religion of then and there but here and now. Second and third and subsequent generations of Christians are not near Jesus of Nazareth, to be sure, but they are near his word and therefore have the blessing of those who have not seen and yet who believe. It is difficult to imagine a point more vital to the life of the church than this. The departure of Jesus and the passing of time do not diminish the availability of effective power. The word is present and abides in the church to accomplish the purposes for which it has been sent.

The Witness of Jesus' Ministry in Conflict with Judaism
(John 5:1—10:42)

A Sabbath Healing—The Lame Man at the Pool
(5:1–47)

The first task for the preacher here as elsewhere is to divide the lengthy narrative into units that have integrity; that is, units which have a single governing focus in an act of Jesus, an event, or a discourse. Discerning where lines may be drawn without violating the text is often a most difficult one in this Gospel. Temporal or geographical references sometimes provide clear clues, but where these are lacking the reader finds sign stories, conversations with Jesus, discourses by Jesus, and theological summaries by the Evangelist flowing without interruption, one into the other. Given the clues we have, this chapter can best be divided into two parts, the sign (vv. 1–18) and the discourse (vv. 19–47), but as we shall note in the discussion below, each of the sections may be helpfully subdivided.

The Sign (5:1–18)

The sign story consists of the sign act (vv. 1–9) and the discussion of the issue aroused by that act (vv. 10–18). The sign itself is related in the fashion to which we are growing accustomed in the book. Except for Jerusalem, the place where the healing occurs is vague, the precise name and location of the pool thus far escaping the historical researcher. The time is "a feast," not necessarily specific since the events that follow have to do, not with a particular feast, but with the Sabbath. The invalid is not unlike others we meet in this Gospel (Jesus' mother, Nicodemus, the Samaritan woman, Martha and Mary) in that expectation of something from Jesus is at one level (aid in getting into the pool), while Jesus responds in a way better than and different from that expectation. Incidentally, the preacher can use the text dispute as to whether v. 4 was in the original account as an occasion to

help listeners appreciate the immense task of those who
strive to provide us with the most reliable text possible. If
such instruction is woven into a sermon on this text, it must
be done clearly, positively, without any hint of "letting laity
in on clergy secrets," and early enough in the message so as
to move briskly on to the central aim of the sermon.

Two lines of thought suggest themselves for preaching
on vv. 1–9. The first has to do with the invalid as a *victim*.
One needs to recognize that some thoughts spawned by the
picture of the pool surrounded by the helpless may sail beyond the intention of the writer. Even so, the victimizing nature of the scene is inescapable. The man who had lain there
38 years, like all the others, was a victim of a kind of religion
that supported a tradition or legend which was inherently
cruel and vicious. They were drawn to the pool with hope of
healing, but the report was that healing came to the person
first to enter the pool after the water was stirred. Imagine all
the false starts and cold plunges on days when brisk winds
gave the effect of an angel's visit to the pool. And suppose an
angel did trouble the water; who would be the *first* to enter?
The paralyzed or severely crippled? Of course not. The prize
would go to someone sufficiently healthy to win the race,
someone with a malady as serious as chapped lips or hang-
nail. The whole fly-swarming, foul-smelling scene is a judgment upon a popular religion that favors the adequate and
sufficient and holds out nothing before those in most extreme
need. Does this sound familiar to anyone?

The second theme in vv. 1–9 worthy of extended attention is the picture of the man as *victor*. Caution must be exer-
cised on two fronts. On the one hand, extensively
psychologizing the story is to be avoided. Jesus' question,
"Do you want to be healed?" does not mean that the man
was a hypochondriac, that he enjoyed poor health, that he
was avoiding the responsibilities that accompany good
health. Such a premise is, of course, fruitful for those who
then interpret Jesus as a master of the power of positive
thinking. The New Testament is not nearly as psychological-
ly oriented as we are. On the other hand, we do not have here
a story of profound faith. At the word of Jesus the man is
healed and he goes his way, not even knowing that the healer
was Jesus (v. 13). This is not an "In the name of Jesus, rise

and walk" story. It is to be remembered that this is a Johannine account and it is, moreover, a sign act; that is to say, it
is a story focusing upon the revelation of God's glory in
Jesus. For the Evangelist, miracles are not presented to underscore the power of faith but to center upon a truth about
God coming to expression in Jesus in whom we have beheld
God's glory. In this Gospel, Jesus acts according to his own
"hour": when and where and how he acts in a revelatory
manner is entirely "from above." All the usual contingencies
and conditions which we customarily associate with Jesus'
benevolent activity—extreme need, persistent faith, and
Jesus' compassion—are subdued to the point of being almost
totally absent in Johannine narratives. The Word from above
is not conditioned by earthly factors, whether it be his mother's request (2:3–4), his brothers' suggestion (7:3–9), his
friends' urgent plea (11:3–6), a crowd's hunger (6:5–6) or the
38-year illness of a man to whom Jesus remained, even after
the healing, a nameless stranger.

How, then, is the invalid a victor? By the act of God's
own free favor. The man is portrayed as totally without a
claim; there is no word as to moral or immoral conduct, no
hint of good or evil deeds, not even a phrase as to faith. He is,
to put it simply, a receiver. The spotlight on this little drama
remains throughout on Jesus, never once sweeping the dark
corners of the stage to find a reason why Jesus acts here,
now, in this way. The reason lies within himself. Can grace
be more radically presented? Even those of us who think we
believe in grace are by this story stripped of everything. In
being so stripped, some of us learn painfully that while
speaking of grace, we have so stressed our faith that it has
become a kind of good work drawing down favor from heav-
en. Grace that is truly grace, needing neither our doubt nor
our faith, is a frightening notion, not simply because it takes
away all claim and calculation, but it forces us back to the
ground of all our being and doing, that God is God.

The issue (vv. 10–18) raised by the healing seems to be
that of sabbath observance, and in some sense that is integral
to the story. No doubt the Johannine church and local synagogues were engaged in the sabbath quarrel and to that
church the message is clear: by the Lord's own word and act,
it is never the wrong day to do the will of God. "My Father is

working still, and I am working" (v. 17). But more is involved than the calendar; otherwise the whole story is a comic tragedy about a man ill for 38 years and healed on the wrong day. What is underlined as central in the sign act is the justification for working on the sabbath. Notice Jesus does not argue that humanitarian claims transcend legal codes ("if an ox falls into the ditch on the sabbath"). Jesus simply points out that the sabbath laws do not apply to God, and since his work and God's work are the same, the law is neither broken nor observed; it does not bear upon his case. The argument is similar to that of Matt 17:24–27 in which Jesus explains that the king's tax does not apply to the king's son.

When the early church confessed Jesus as Son of God they were, therefore, not only affirming that he liberated those victimized by a popular religion which gave no help to those totally helpless, but he also set persons free from legalism. The law which prescribed what *persons* could and could not do had become in the hands of some religionists a definition of what *God* could and could not do. Healing a man on the sabbath is a punishable crime because the law is the law and even God must abide by the rules. Once you begin allowing for exceptions, their carefully constructed house of religion will collapse. The alternatives before the opponents of Jesus are quite clear: either re-think their position on the law and acknowledge God has been manifested in the cure, or hold firmly their view and reject the healer, the healing, and the healed. Their decision is not unique in the history of religious strife and persecution.

It should not be unnoticed by the preacher that the healed man was arrested for obeying Jesus. This Gospel points out repeatedly (the blind man, chap. 9; Lazarus, chap. 11) that those who are recipients of Jesus' benefits suffer along with Jesus. In the farewell discourses (chaps. 14–16) this theme will be amply emphasized: those whose lives are touched by Jesus must bear the animosity of the world as did Jesus. One does not *use* Jesus to make one's life a success story (good health, happiness, prosperity) but one assumes discipleship as a burden as well as a blessing. In fact, the charge of blasphemy hurled at Jesus for calling God his Father (v. 18) was no less a charge against the church which confessed Jesus as Son of God. Reading and hearing these texts in which there was cost to discipleship do not find their adequate fulfillment in us by our wishing for martyrdom or at least finding new ways to observe Lent. The fact is, Christian confessions and convictions are still met with resistance when spoken or acted upon outside the circles of supportive amens. It is probably true that more Christians around the world have suffered imprisonment and death in this generation than in the generation during which this Gospel was written. It is easier to idealize the past than to live faithfully in the present.

The Discourse (5:19–47)

The discourse section of this chapter actually consists of two discourses. The first (vv. 19–29) grows out of the discussion of the Son's oneness with the Father which immediately precedes this unit. However, the healing itself has now totally receded, as is the nature of miracles treated as signs; the act itself serves primarily to launch a revelation discourse. Those students in search of "only the facts" are left in a twilight zone of unanswered questions. In fact, the healing has now so completely disappeared that anyone reading vv. 19–29 would assume the discourse followed a raising from the dead rather than a healing of the lame. Life and death, judgment and resurrection are the categories governing this section.

The person who preaches through this Gospel will want to be thorough in treating major themes but at the same time avoid unnecessary repetition. This Gospel repeats without variation and repeats with variation some of its major lines of thought. Judgment and eternal life constitute an often treated subject, with two accents, present and future. How one treats the text before us will be determined in part by the particular approach taken earlier in messages on 3:16–21 and 3:31–36, especially 3:36. It is quite clear that 5:24 underlines the present, realized dimension of eschatology. Judgment is that crisis, that moment when one is encountered by the word of Christ which is met with unbelief or belief. If the response is faith, judgment is past and one is living the eternal life. Because this present, here and now emphasis appears so repeatedly in this Gospel one has to assume this was the message most needed in the Johannine church. Perhaps some were postponing life, denying this present existence, and hiding in some form of futurism. Each preacher will determine the extent to which that problem continues in his or her community and how often to address it. This Gospel is the New Testament's best resource for such efforts, even though Paul often makes very similar statements (for example, Rom 5:1; 6:13; Col 2:12—3:1).

However, there is little doubt that 5:28–29 refers to future judgment and resurrection. Scholars have accounted for these verses in a variety of ways. Did the Evangelist include both perspectives to satisfy both sides of a debate in the church? Did the Evangelist include this closing sentence to guard against tendencies toward over-realized eschatology? Or did a later editor in the Johannine church add this word about the future to help bring the community into harmony with the more "orthodox" perspective of the church at large? The commentaries will reflect and defend these and other positions. The fact remains that both present and future dimensions of judgment and eternal life are found in the Gospel as we have it. There is no reason why both cannot exist meaningfully in the faith of the church, the one or the other receiving attention whenever overemphasis leads to distortion of faith and diminishes the fullness of Christian living.

The second and distinctly separate discourse in vv. 30–47 consists of a line of witnesses testifying that Jesus truly was sent from God. The list is quite impressive: John the Baptist, God, Jesus' works, the Scriptures, and Moses. The preacher might be tempted to deliver a message persuading the listeners as though they were a jury or reconfirming the listeners who have already been persuaded. However, the line of witnesses presented here was more impressive to the Johannine church than to a modern one. The three significant communities in the writer's world are the church, the synagogue, and the sect of John the Baptist. This list of witnesses is a way of saying all three testify that Jesus is of God: John the Baptist for that group, Moses and Scripture for the synagogue, and Jesus' works and God (perhaps a reference to the divine voice at Jesus' baptism) as the witnesses offered by the church. Repeating this argument in the church today would be less than meaningful. Unless followers of Moses or of John the Baptist are real and present factors in the definition of the Christian faith in one's community, then an alternative way to present 5:30–47 should be chosen.

One might well choose to do in our time and place what this Evangelist did in his. The writer chose the most impressive witnesses available to strengthen and instruct the church. To achieve the same end today, where would one look for testimonies as effective? They would have to be, if the pattern of our text is to be followed, witnesses both within the church and outside, both supporting the Gospel and opposed to it. Would it not be biblical preaching in a genuine sense if one were to attempt for one's listeners what the Fourth Evangelist accomplished for his?

Perhaps more effective, however, would be a message that probes the question raised by the text: Why were the witnesses not believed? Why did so few move to faith in Jesus as a result of their testimony? The charge against those who heard the witnesses but without faith are as follows:

(1) They embraced the witnesses, idolized them, and hence robbed them of their purposes. Consider, for example, John the Baptist. Just as it was customary in that day to place torches along the way to point people to some great occasion, so John was a torch burning and shining (v. 35). What happened? The hearers rejoiced in his light for awhile (v. 35). They enjoyed his sermons, commented favorably on his style and delivery, approved of his messages as good speeches, and remarked upon how superior he was to some they had heard. The preacher thus being put in the center, the preaching was robbed of power and purpose. John was elevated to become a competitor of the one to whom he witnessed. This particular sin seems to have grown in popularity. Or consider the witness of Scripture. The Scriptures, says the writer, find their proper purpose in pointing to Christ. But what happened? The Bible was embraced and studied diligently on the assumption that knowledge of Bible verses gave life (v. 39). Such adoration of Scripture continues to hinder their proper function. While it is rather common to have someone rail against those secularists who have rejected the Christian faith, no less serious and perhaps more serious a problem is the idolatrous embrace of all the persons, events, occasions, texts, experiences, places, traditions and institutions which have as their primary purpose turn-

ing people to God. And tragically this perversion seldom
comes under judgment because it appears as faithfulness in
supporting those very persons, traditions, and institutions
that bear God's name. John the Baptist had great crowds;
who would knock that? Who among us wishes to speak
against Bible study? And would a gift to endow the church
building be rejected? Of course not! Then what is the problem? Sin is often so insidious as to kill by embrace.

(2) The listeners to the witness had already formed a
tight circle of mutuality, giving, receiving, agreeing, confirming, complimenting, and securing each other. A voice, a witness from outside that circle would not be received as a word
from God. The closing verses of the chapter (vv. 41–47) make
it clear that Jesus will not be received as one sent from God.
The reason is simple: he is not one of them. In fact, how can
any new and fresh word from God come to those who already
possess it so certainly? Of course, one is not expected to be so
open as to follow any and every stranger who speaks God's
name, but one is called upon at least to listen. The believing
community is not left totally vulnerable to every itinerant
preacher, every passing wonder worker; Scripture, tradition,
and reason provide discerning ears. But to conclude *before*
and not *after* listening is to replace open trust with closed
fear. And when that condition prevails, whether one is speaking of church or society, violence soon follows. One already
senses, therefore, in chapter 5 the approaching arrest and execution of Jesus.

A Passover Sign—Feeding the Multitudes (6:1–71)

Two matters will be discussed by the major commentaries which, while seeming not to bear directly upon sermons
on this chapter, will give to the preacher a reservoir of
knowledge about this section out of which confidence and
courage for preaching are born. Nothing is so erosive of good
preaching as uncertainty due to lack of study. The first matter has to do with the possible mislocation of chapter 6. The
reader of the Fourth Gospel notices that chapter 4 ends with
Jesus in Galilee, chapter 5 is set in Jerusalem, chapter 6 takes
place in Galilee, and in chapter 7 Jesus returns to Jerusalem.
Geography alone argues that chapters 4, 6, 5, 7 would be a
more reasonable sequence. But this presupposes an interest

in itineraries and chronology on the part of the writer. No
Greek text we possess has the narrative in any order other
than the present one, but even those who have abandoned
reconstructing a life of Jesus are nevertheless still teased into
a bit of it.

A second and more directly pertinent consideration is
the linking in chapter 6 of the feeding of the 5000, walking on
the water and the confession of Simon Peter. Matthew
(14:13-27) and Mark (6:32-51) have the feeding and walking
on water in adjoining pericopae with the confession of Simon
Peter shortly thereafter (Matt 16:13-20; Mark 8:27-30). Luke
omits the walking on water but joins directly the feeding and
Simon's confession (9:10-22). Whatever one may conclude
about the relation of this Gospel to the Synoptics, it seems
most likely that these three stories had already been joined
in the tradition prior to the work of this Evangelist. That the
feeding and the walking on water were already one narrative
is without question. While we shall discuss them separately,
it will be clear to the preacher that the two should be treated
as one unit for the purpose of preaching. That they belong
together is not solely a literary judgment but a theological
one.

The Feeding (6:1-15)

The story is set in the hills on the other side of the Sea of
Galilee. The time is Passover, which may be more of a theological reference than a temporal one. In chapter 2 at Passover time Jesus spoke of his death after cleansing the Temple.
In 13:1 at Passover Jesus knows it is his hour to die. So here
in this chapter the eucharistic language of Jesus' flesh and
blood causes the reader to sense that the story is more than
an account of feeding the hungry. Noticeably absent also is
the description of Jesus' compassion on the hungry crowds as
is so prominent in the Synoptic accounts. Here rather is the
matter of fact statement after a question testing Philip: "for
he himself knew what he would do" (v. 6). There are the usual Johannine clues that Jesus will perform a sign that will
provide something qualitatively better than what is expected. Recall the sign on the occasion of a shortage of wine
in chapter 2. For the preacher to dip into the Synoptics to
pick up the "compassion on the hungry" theme would be to

miss the Evangelist's point. The writer insists that the reader look beyond the bread to the Bread.

The crowds are there, drawn by having seen signs, but so did they gather in Jerusalem because of signs (2:23–25). And just as Jesus did not trust those in Jerusalem who so responded, neither does he here. Good attendance does not say in itself anything about the intrinsic value of a gathering. And even though the crowd, now fully fed, proclaims Jesus to be the prophet like Moses who was to come (Deut 18:18), it is not enough. In fact, Jesus retreats before the crowd's efforts to take their future into their own hands and set Jesus up as king (v. 15). It is the usual ugly scene of enthroning those who do things for us, putting a chicken in every pot and a car in every garage. But Jesus knows what we sometimes forget, that popularity can be as dangerous as hostility.

In sum, the story thus far may be simply stated: as Moses fed the multitude in the wilderness, so did Jesus. Were this the end of the matter, then the crowd seems to have judged correctly: "This is indeed the prophet who is to come into the world!" (v. 14).

Walking on Water (6:16–21)

As stated earlier, the preacher will want to avoid isolating this story and preaching on it separately. Usually such sermons show little more than the speaker's fondness for the spectacular, achieve little more than bragging on Jesus, and may even spawn questions about Jesus using his power to make trips easier or to take short cuts. The fact is, this story is a companion to the feeding account. In the exodus tradition, mastery over the sea and feeding the people in the wilderness had long been joined. Note, for example, the recitation in Psalm 78 of God's caring for Israel. In the New Testament, Paul recalls for the Corinthian church the experiences of Israel at the sea and in the wilderness feedings, comparing those events to baptism and the eucharist (1 Cor 10:1–5). We have in two stories the clear association of Jesus with Moses and by implication it presents the achievement of Jesus as a new exodus for his people. The account of Jesus walking on the sea has its own center in the word of Jesus to his followers, "I am" (v. 20). By using the name of God in this way, the

tradition here agrees with Mark and Matthew in treating
this event as a theophany.

The Discourse on Bread (6:22–59)

There likely will be little loss for the pulpit and no compromise of the message of this section if the preacher refrains
from attempting to isolate layers and strands of tradition.
There will be occasions for teaching in the parish in which
such exercises into which some commentaries lead us can be
entered into with profit. By the time we reach this point in
the Gospel we have already become aware that the Evangelist has the Christian reader in mind much more than he does
the Galilean crowd. Even so, these verses are offered as the
discourse of Jesus in a synagogue in Capernaum to the multitude from whom he had fled the day before.

The discourse opens with the typically Johannine two-
level use of language, the crowd clamoring for more and better bread while Jesus calls for trusting reception of the life-
giving word from heaven. Resisting Jesus' claim to have been
sent from God, the crowd demands from Jesus some proof
supporting the claim, some credential that would put him in
Moses' category. The line of argument is the same as that of
the Samaritan woman: are you greater than Jacob? It is important for the interpreter not to move too quickly in assuming that the true bread from heaven, the bread of God which
gives life to the world (vv. 32–33) is Jesus in a eucharistic
sense. That is yet to come, probably no earlier than v. 48.
Until that point, the references to Jesus as bread from above
could well be referring to him as the Logos, the Word. Notice
the discussion of being *taught* of God, *hearing* and *learning*
from God (v. 45). These support the interpretation of the first
part of the discourse (vv. 22–47) as referring to Jesus as the
revealing Word of God, as in the Prologue. Philo of Alexan-
dria had earlier called the manna the Wisdom or Word of
God. He did so as a commentary upon Deut 8:3 which asserts
that God fed Israel with manna from heaven in order to remind the people that "man shall not live by bread alone, but
by every word that proceeds from the mouth of God." The
manna, said Philo, is that word from God. Such a handling of
our present text is altogether sound and enables the Evangelist and the modern preacher to move past a Moses–Jesus

competition over who provides the best feast in the wilderness.

The chapter began with provision of bread, but even then with clues that more than bread was involved since Jesus had in mind from the outset a "sign" pointing beyond bread to Bread. Earlier he had pointed beyond birth to Birth (chap. 3) and beyond water to Water (chap. 4). And so from the opening provision of bread the story has moved to Jesus as the Bread in the sense of the lifegiving Word from heaven. No preacher should let slip this opportunity to develop the theme of the hunger behind and beneath all other hungers, the longing for a knowledge of God, a word from God. Jesus understood this and so was able to resist the wilderness tempter's lure into something less, the turning of stones to bread. "Man shall not live by bread alone" (Matt 4:4). The worst of all famines, warned the prophets, would be a famine of the word of God. From Adam until now, there has been no question more fundamentally human than this: "Is there any word from God?" "Break Thou the Bread of Life," is a hymn intended to precede not the eucharist but the sermon.

However, the talk of bread from heaven does, at v. 48 or at least v. 51, become clearly eucharistic. The language of vv. 11 and 23 earlier was noticeably eucharistic but not nearly so bold and predictably offensive as it now becomes through v. 59. The offense lies at two points of identification. The first is Jesus' association of himself with God rather than Moses. Had Jesus been content to be the fulfillment of the promise for a prophet like Moses to arise (Deut 18:18), then the crowd's earlier confession (v. 14) would have been accepted as adequate faith. But in the Johannine church, as we have seen, the fully adequate faith does not view Jesus as the fulfillment of Jewish expectations of the prophet or even of the Messiah. He does fulfill those to be sure, but he did that at the first and most elementary level of this narrative—giving bread in the wilderness. But that was a "sign," meaning that more than expected and better than expected were being signified. The story moves, therefore, beyond Moses the giver of bread to God the real giver, and here Jesus identifies himself with the Father (vv. 41–46).

The preacher will want to think carefully here about Christology. For example, Matthew and Luke seem satisfied

to present a Christ who fulfills the promises and prophecies
of Israel. This Gospel, however, like the Epistle to the
Hebrews, is concerned to show the superiority of Christianity
over Judaism and therefore presents a Christ who not only
fulfills but who even transcends the categories of prophecy–fulfillment. In Hebrews, for example, Moses was a servant in the house; the Christ as Son is lord over the house
(3:3–6). Essentially the same argumentation is in our present
text. In Hebrews, Judaism is to Christianity as shadow is to
substance (8:5; 9:25; 10:1); in the Gospel of John, the relationship is that of the apparent and the real (6:32,58). Now
the question facing the preacher here is a decision as to
whether to look at those New Testament sources for Christology which have sought to emphasize continuity with Judaism (Luke, and in a real sense also Matt), or to those who
have hammered out a Christology *over against* Judaism (John
and Hebrews). Whichever path is taken, the preacher should
be aware of the difference and the conditions under which
these early views of Christ were reached. Such awareness
shall then help self-critically as one tries to be honest in the
admission that likewise our images of Christ contains elements of continuity with both tradition and culture as well
as elements of opposition to both tradition and culture. To
admit that faith's portrait of Christ contains old and new,
both embrace and rejection, is to confess one's faith more
humbly and to hear other Christians more openly.

The other point of identification which is offensive to
hearers is that of calling himself the bread to be eaten (vv.
51–59). The writer had to know that pressing the image of
Jesus as bread into the eucharistic language of eating flesh
and drinking blood was so radical as to be offensive not
only to Jews but also to some Christians who found this a
hard saying (v. 60) and who could no longer follow him (v.
66). It is one thing to take the eucharistic bread and wine
and recall that it is himself that Christ gives for the life of
the world; it is another to say that we are to eat his flesh
and drink his blood. The New Testament probably offers no
more shocking way of saying that Jesus Christ is not like
Moses, giving the people something from God. Rather, in
Jesus Christ, God is coming to us and giving life for life, and
by our participation we have life in ourselves. We abide in

God and God abides in us, says the eucharist of the Johannine church.

The Responses (6:60–71)

The Jewish listeners rejected the sermon in the synagogue at Capernaum. And interestingly enough, the writer
acknowledges that some Christians also found it offensive. In
other words, the Johannine church held a position which was
not shared by all Christian groups. It is unrealistic when
reading the New Testament to think of only two groups, Jews
and Christians. As there were differing groups within Judaism (Pharisees, Sadducees, Essenes, *et al.*) so there were different communities of Christian believers, perhaps finding
their identity in the person and teaching of an apostle or
other leader. In these verses, as one observes a crumbling of
that group referred to as "disciples," some by theological disagreement and one by betrayal, Simon Peter makes a confession of faith for the group that remains. It is a group or
church confession: notice the use of "we" (v. 68). Although
the confession is different from that of the Synoptics, it is
again Simon Peter who makes it.

Throughout this chapter one thing has been said repeatedly which is the real offense behind all the other offenses
and is, in fact, the offense of all Scripture: we have life by the
election of grace. It may be said gently: the bread God gives
from heaven provides life to the world. It may be said bluntly
so as to offend all our claims of free will: no one comes to me
except the Father draw him. However it may be stated, this
is the point of contact and often of conflict: do we determine
our own lives or does God? In every paragraph the audience
of Jesus wants to preside. They demand that he do what
Moses did; they want proofs so that they will have adequate
reasons to conclude that Jesus is from God (intellectual
works righteousness); they will have Jesus be king if they so
determine and then elevate him as such. But repeatedly, in a
variety of images and analogies, Jesus says one thing: life is
from heaven as a gift; trust this and life is yours. It had been
said earlier to Nicodemus who was asking what to do and
how to do it. Salvation is "from above." That message is not
so difficult to understand as it is difficult to accept, cutting
across, as it does, all our calculations and achievements.

The subject of chapter 6, then, is grace, or perhaps more clearly in our language, gift. The bread in the wilderness was a gift. The bread as word from heaven was and is a gift. The bread on the table of the eucharist is a gift. What does one do, standing thus before the gift?

A Disturbing Appearance at the Feast of Tabernacles (7:1–52)

Upon first reading, this chapter may seem to offer little for preaching that has not been dealt with in earlier events or discourses. And it is most certainly true that one finds here several already familiar themes concerning the person of Jesus, who he is and what he is doing. However, new constellations of old material create different perspectives and hence provide fresh insight. For example, the conversations and speeches of this chapter have as their setting the Feast of Tabernacles or Tents. This festival, originally associated with autumn harvest, was re-interpreted in Israel's history as a festival recalling the days of pilgrim life in the wilderness. Tents or booths or brush arbors were constructed and in them Jewish families spent time, remembering the way of life of their ancestors. Since we have already seen that Passover is with this Evangelist more a theological than a chronological reference, so we can expect Tabernacles to provide a clue to understanding Jesus' words to the worshipers in Jerusalem.

A second key to understanding chapter 7 is the theological distance between Galilee and Judea. We tend to think of the entire area as "Israel," but since the return from exile, Judea in the south was the center of the nation's religious life, for here was Jerusalem, and in Jerusalem, the temple. In fact, "Judaism" received its name from Judah. The word "Jews," found so often in this book, is an almost slang translation of the Greek word "Judeans." (An explanation of the word "Jews" is necessary at 7:1 in order for it to make sense.) Galilee, on the other hand, was regarded as marginal in terms of orthodox Judaism. In Galilee resided many non-Jews, and compromises of the faith in matters of food laws, sabbath-keeping, and ritual purification were not uncommon. That Jesus was from Galilee and that Galilee provided a refuge

from death threats in Judea are statements of significance
far beyond geographical distinctions.

A third key to this chapter lies in the identification of the
two major groups which respond to Jesus, and in the relationship generated by those responses. There is the crowd
from whom Jesus received mixed reviews: belief, doubt, uncertainty and confusion. And there are the religious leaders,
priests and Pharisees who oppose Jesus, seeking his arrest
and death. But even among these there is disagreement, as
the case of Nicodemus discloses (vv. 50–52). In addition,
there is a great deal of interchange, filled with doubt, suspicion and anger between the crowd and the leaders. To these
dynamics we shall return shortly.

Introduction: Jesus and His Brothers (7:1–13)

The brothers of Jesus figure here only in the discussion of
Jesus' movement from the safety of Galilee to the dangers of
Judea. The account is reminiscent of the Cana wedding story
(2:1–12) in which the brothers are mentioned but only Jesus'
mother receives attention. As at Cana, a suggestion is made
to Jesus, Jesus rejects the suggestion on the grounds that his
time has not come, and then Jesus acts as though he were
following the suggestion. However, what Jesus actually does
and what is suggested are really quite different. Again, as at
Cana, the word of Jesus to his family seems abrupt and
harsh. In fact, Greek manuscripts differ as to whether Jesus
told his brothers he was *not* going up to the feast or *not yet*
going up to the feast (v. 8). The more difficult *not* is more
likely the original. In either case, we do not know in what
mood the brothers suggested Jesus move out of obscurity in
Galilee and go public in Jerusalem at a time when crowds
would be large. While they were not believers in Jesus, they
were not necessarily cynical.

What is the Evangelist saying to the church in this brief
exchange between Jesus and his brothers? We do not know in
what regard Jesus' immediate family was held in the Johannine community, but it is not likely that there was any need
to disabuse the church of any misplaced loyalty or adoration
toward the family of Jesus. If any error needed correction it
would more likely be that of assuming those persons in close
proximity to Jesus had a distinct advantage over believers of

another time and place. Such thinking, that "back then they had Jesus; today we only have the writings about him," could certainly produce a church with low self-esteem and a self-defeating attitude. The fact of the matter is, says the writer, there was no advantage to being there and then. Even members of Jesus' own family did not believe in him. The sources, the grounds, the risks, the nature of faith have not changed. When Jesus was on earth one could see and not see, hear and not hear. One recalls here Mark 3:31–35 as a comparison to this text. During a busy day of ministering, Jesus was told that his mother and brothers were outside, asking for him. "And he replied, 'Who are my mother and my brothers?' And looking around on those who sat about him, he said, 'Here are my mother and my brothers! Whoever does the will of God is my brother, and sister, and mother.' "

Equally unavoidable is the message to the church in the words of Jesus to his brothers: "My time has not yet come, but your time is always here. The world cannot hate you, but it hates me because I testify of it that its works are evil" (vv. 6–7). The church is not to be surprised to find itself the object of hatred in the world. That comes with discipleship. Jesus did not come to condemn the world but the truth on his lips precipitated crises and drew to Jesus the ire of those who felt under judgment because of their behavior. In the very real sense of the word, Jesus "made a difference" in the world. Speaking the truth in circumstances where prejudice, greed, hatred, and injustice not only prevail but often receive religious blessing does make a difference. Making a difference is painful and only the distorted enjoy pain. But the church which knows its own time will speak and do the truth and bear the consequences. But woe to the church of whom it can be said, "It is always your time. What you say and do does not really make any difference, because you do not witness to the truth. The world does not hate you because it has no reason to do so. You are not really a factor in the destiny of the world." Jesus says to the church, "Some claim to be my relatives; some claim to be my friends; some brag that I once preached in their town; but *you* are my disciples." If Paul were writing this paragraph he would say that if the world hates you, "it has been granted to you that for the sake of Christ you should not only believe in him but also suffer for his sake" (Phil 1:29). Hopefully, it is not necessary to remind ourselves that there is a difference between being hated for Christ's sake and being hated for one's obnoxious religiosity.

Jesus Receives Mixed Responses (7:14-52)

This chapter makes it clear that from the multitude Jesus received affirmative, negative, and uncertain responses. There is in this nothing surprising or unusual. Faith is not now nor was it ever coerced, even by the physical presence of Jesus. A Yes is a meaningful Yes only where a No is possible. However, in areas of our culture where Christianity is so widely accepted, a No is often met with intolerance, as though the presence of a No weakened or cast doubt upon our Yes. Apparently the Yes must be unanimous! Some Christians therefore create the illusion of a unanimous Yes by living in faith ghettos in which they can witness to one another without fear of question or contradiction.

One of the painful dimensions of these reports of responses to Jesus is the distance between lay and clergy members in the community. The lay folk are suspicious of the clergy: why do the leaders let Jesus speak openly? Could it be that they really believe him to be the Christ (vv. 25-27)? And conversely, the clergy do not trust the people to make their own decisions: Why are you being led astray? Look at us clergy; you do not see us following Jesus, do you (vv. 47-48)? In fact, the clergy had already put down the laity under the broad stereotype of ignorant and accursed (v. 49). The religious leaders had studied their Bibles, drawn their conclusions about the who, what and where of the promised Messiah, and the case was closed without need for hearing the evidence (vv. 50-52). Their systems and categories were fixed and final; there was no way the word of God would come as a surprise; there would be no returning to the theological drawing board. With such unhealthy relationships existing within and between the lay and clergy communities, it is no surprise that there erupted in the midst of doubt, belief and uncertainty a strong hatred toward Jesus and a desire to be rid of him. His presence brought into the open the diseased condition of the community's spirit.

A most important issue arises in this chapter which is central to all proclamation: "How is faith generated?" We have had several occasions to notice that demands for proofs, on the grounds that subsequent to adequate proofs would come faith, have been rejected. The accent has been upon witnessing rather than upon proving. And now here the handling of "evidence" by the people is pathetic if not ridiculous. Some believe because they cannot imagine anyone doing more signs than Jesus. Note the assumption: the one doing the most signs is the Messiah (v. 31). Some disbelieved because they knew Jesus to be from Galilee and the Messiah is supposed to have a mysterious origin (v. 27). Others disbelieved because they knew the Messiah was to be from Bethlehem, David's city, and Jesus was from Galilee (vv. 42–43). It is striking that if this Evangelist knew the birth stories he does not use them to prove anything. While Matthew and Luke found it useful to relate the Bethlehem stories to confirm if not generate belief that Jesus was indeed the promised Messiah, this writer makes no such attempt. Obviously faith is understood to be more than the response of the mind to the evidence. Judging proofs to be adequate or inadequate, developing arguments, designing syllogisms: these are, for the Fourth Evangelist, "of the earth." Faith is born of revelation and no one comes except by being drawn of God.

Does this Gospel then render the listener totally passive to the witnessing, stripped of responsibility? No. Insight into the nature of one's response to the witness is provided by the words of Jesus in vv. 16–17: "My teaching is not mine but his who sent me; if any man's will is to do his will, he shall know whether the teaching is from God or whether I am speaking on my own authority." The path to knowing God, to understanding the witness, to beholding the glory, is willingness to obey God's will. The formula is simple: one who will not, cannot. In Matthean language (in a passage often called a Johannine flight into Matthew), one takes the yoke and learns, one does not learn in order to decide whether to take the yoke (Matt 11:29). One can, of course, locate so much of one's religion in the will that a volitional distortion results. But after duly warning ourselves about the frailties and limits of the human will, there remains the truth that *willingness to do* opens doors locked to the casual, the curious and the passerby.

The evangelist tells us there were conversations and disputes during the Feast of Tabernacles. What irony! The community of faith has gathered for that festival celebrating their history as a pilgrim people, living in tents, having no abiding city, with no compass but trust in God. These people whose past was nothing, who were no people, slaves in Egypt; these people whose future was uncertain save for the certainty of trust; these are the people who will evaluate Jesus only in terms of his past and future. These people who had neither unless they claim God as their past and future, now reject Jesus because he claims God as his past and his future. Jesus says he comes from God (vv. 28–29); they say he comes from Galilee and that is not an adequate past. Jesus says he is going again to God (vv. 33–34); they say he must be going to live among the Gentiles (vv. 35–36) and that is an inadequate future. The one who epitomized what Tabernacles memorialized, pilgrimage from God to God, was not recognized by those assembled for the week of remembering. It is shocking and painful when "they" become "we" in the realization that groups can and do continue to assemble long after they have forgotten the whence, whither, and why.

Perhaps a word needs to be said about the very important invitation of Jesus for any who thirsts to come and drink, and the promise of the Spirit which would be in the believer as a flowing spring (vv. 37–39). This image associating water and the Spirit is familiar not only from earlier stories in this Gospel (ch. 3-4), but also from Isa 44:1–5. But familiarity alone does not justify preaching on this text at this point. The text itself points forward to the time when the Son will be glorified (the Johannine expression for the death, resurrection, ascension of Christ) and from the presence of God will send to his followers the Holy Spirit (16:7). It seems wise, therefore, to hold this passage in reserve until we come to the promise of the Spirit in the farewell discourses and to the giving of the Spirit by the glorified Christ (20:22). But it is not too soon to fix firmly in mind three matters upon which the writer will repeatedly insist: the Spirit is a gift to the followers of Jesus; the gift is from Jesus; the gift is from Jesus upon his glorification. To these matters we will return.

Discussions in the Temple (7:53—8:59)

Chapter 8 continues the narrative of the preceding chapter: the scene is Jerusalem, the subject is the person of Jesus, the characters are Jesus, the crowd and the religious leaders, the mood ranges from general confusion to fierce hostility, and the conclusion is clearly predictable—Jesus will be put to death. However, Jesus is not yet arrested. The reason given for his continuing at large is sometimes theological (his time had not yet come, v. 20) and sometimes historical (Jesus hid and then left the area, v. 59). The major portion of this section consists of rather loosely joined accounts of clashes between Jesus and the Jews over the question of whether Jesus is really from God. For purposes of discussion and presentation these conflicts may be divided into three units. However, before those can be examined, some decisions have to be made about 7:53–8:11.

Jesus and the Adulteress (7:53–8:11)

The minister of a congregation cannot overlook the fact that the presence of 7:53–8:11 in the Gospel is highly problematic. Parishioners in their own Bible reading will notice how different translations signal the uncertainties. Some may even notice that the RSV put the passage in the footnotes in the 1946 edition and then returned it to the text in the 1971 edition, offering a brief note about its questionable status. But the minister does not just respond to issues that are noticed by the congregation; the minister is a leader and as such, takes initiative. There are primarily two settings available for helping the church deal with 7:53–8:11. The more appropriate for this kind of work is the teaching context. Here one can move thoughtfully through the overwhelming evidence that the account has a non-Johannine origin. It is absent from early manuscripts, it interrupts the continuity of 7:52 and 8:12, it is different in vocabulary and style, and in Greek manuscripts of the New Testament it has been variously located: here, or after 7:36, or after 7:44, or after 21:25, or after Luke 21:38. The story has Luke's focus on forgiveness and lacks this Gospel's customary revelation discourse. One could also explain that the familiarity of the church with this story and the obvious antiquity of the ac-

count have caused many scholars who doubt the propriety of
its present location to consent to continuing it as a part of
this Gospel as long as the readers are alerted to the
problems. The minister as teacher can use this occasion to
help the church understand the work and difficulties of providing a copy of the New Testament. If done honestly and
patiently such instruction gives the Bible to the church with
new appreciation rather than taking it away with unsettling
doubts.

The pulpit in the worship setting does not allow the time
or the dynamic for much work with textual problems. All sermons hopefully have some instructional force, but this may
be too much for a sermon to bear. But even if the attention
were given to the problems surrounding 7:53–8:11, one
would still have to decide whether it should be the text of a
sermon. Even the belief that the account records an actual
event from Jesus' ministry does not decide favorably as to its
being a preaching text. We do not preach on "things that really happened, in or out of the Bible"; we preach from texts
which the church has called Scripture. One can hardly hold
at the same time that a text is spurious and that it is Scripture. Were one to decide to preach on the passage, it would
be wise not to do so as a part of a series on this Gospel. That
the story is non-Johannine is evident to any careful reader of
the other accounts in this Gospel of those things Jesus said
and did.

Jesus as Light (8:12–20)

There are perhaps no passages more seductive for
preachers than the "I am's" of the Fourth Gospel. "I am the
light of the world" (v. 12) is no exception. The expression
sounds so unambiguously good and positive and right. All
that is left for the preacher to do, it seems, is to think of the
ways light is such a blessing in our lives and then transfer the
benefits of the analogy to Jesus. But care in reading the text
convinces us otherwise.

The images of light and darkness are not new here; they
have been introduced before (1:5, 9; 3:19) in the discussions
of God's lifegiving revelation. Nor are they peculiar to this
Gospel. Judaism, in countless canonical and non-canonical
texts, spoke of God, of Torah, and even of the people of Israel

as light. And other religions have freely employed these images to distinguish between true and false, good and evil, life and death. Since the Feast of Tabernacles provides the theological if not chronological framework for Jesus' discourse, it may be that Israel's recollection of the guiding fire by night during those tabernacle years lies in the immediate background of this text. However, such association is not essential for its understanding. What is essential is the text's direct connection between light and judgment. Light has its life-giving, encouraging and clarifying functions, to be sure, but in the context here, as was the case at 3:19–21, light has a penetrating, discriminating and judging force. Again it needs to be repeated: the light is not *for the purpose of* judging, as though there were in God some fiendish delight in switching on the light in a cellar full of cockroaches. But even so, light does come as judgment upon those who prefer darkness. The point is, with the availability of light, darkness is now a choice.

And what is it to live in such darkness? We deceive ourselves if we think of primitive people in the "dark" remote areas of the world, still without digital watches and microwave ovens. We deceive ourselves if we think only of derelicts crawling along the "dark" alley ways of our cities. It is also darkness to refuse to hear the truth and to tolerate no teacher or preacher or politician who tells it. It is to avoid certain sections of town so as not to be disturbed by the conditions in which some have to live. It is to avoid any book or any speaker who shatters my illusions of innocence in this evil world. It is not to ask questions at work, at home, or at church because I prefer to let sleeping dogs lie. It is to persuade myself that problems in the church, in the schools, in the neighborhood, in society at large are really none of my business. No wonder, then, that sermons on God's love for the world come into such darkness as judging light. That Jesus' presentation of himself as light for the world should create opposition among those who held heavy investments in darkness comes really as no surprise at all.

It will be left to each reader of these comments to ascertain what element of truth there may be in the recent criticisms of preaching as severely lacking in terms of bringing the light of truth about God and the human condition into dark places. Some concerned Christians have sensed that the church and its ministers have become so heavily psychologized in recent years that we are experiencing a subjective captivity of the Gospel. Perhaps. It certainly is true that one does not have to travel far to hear a sermon on "How to Grow Accustomed to the Dark." Whoever would preach from the Fourth Gospel must first come to grips with certain unavoidable presuppositions of the book: there is love and there is hatred; there is light and there is darkness; there is life and there is death.

Jesus as Son of God (8:21–30)

An early step in sermon preparation is the determination of the limits of a text: where does the unit properly begin and end? At times this is difficult to determine; at other times, quite easy. Here the task is quite easy, for v. 21 obviously is a beginning and v. 30 is a conclusion. If the material in between sounds familiar it is because of the very close parallel in 7:32–36. Some have judged these to be two forms of the same scene. But the differences are certainly worth attention. For example, both contain the typical misunderstanding in response to Jesus' comments about his approaching departure. In 7:32–36, the listeners wonder if Jesus is going among the Greeks; in 8:22 they wonder if he is going to kill himself. The two responses illustrate a characteristic of this Gospel which will be increasingly evident as the narrative progresses. Persons around Jesus who do not understand or believe or who may even be enemies will sometimes say unwittingly what is near the truth, if not the truth. In fact, these comments function in the narrative as prophecies. Jesus will become available to the Greeks in his death and ascension (12:20–26). Jesus will not kill himself but he will lay down his life for the sheep (10:11–15). The same phenomenon will appear in Mary's anointing Jesus, not knowing it is for his burial (12:1–7) and in Caiaphas' political assessment that "it is expedient for you that one man should die for the people, and that the whole nation should not perish" (11:50), not knowing the truth he spoke.

If this seems strange to us who breathe in an atmosphere of free will and intentionality, two reminders may be helpful. In its declaration of the sovereignty of God in the world, the

Bible often affirms that God's purposes are carried out by
persons, nations and events in ways far beyond the inten-
tions of those involved. So did the story of Joseph and his
brothers transcend the spite and envy of the brothers who
sold Joseph into Egypt. Cyrus of Persia (Isa 45:1) surely was
not aware that God was using him as "an anointed one," a
shepherd to effect the restoration of Israel. Whatever the mo-
tives and reasons that prompted Judas, he was responsible
for them and for the act of treachery which followed. And yet
God used this ugliest of deeds for our salvation. That this
Gospel offers cases of persons speaking more truth than they
know is not, then, a perspective foreign to Scripture as a
whole. The second reminder is that this Gospel characteristi-
cally tells its story "from above," emphasizing God's revelation, God's time and place, God's initiative, God's call.
Especially as the narrative moves closer to the death of
Jesus, the writer will remind the reader on every page that
what appears on the historical level to be political and social
machination is really much more than that. God is God and
is able to work the divine purpose through what was intended otherwise. There will be occasions to return more than
once to this troubling but encouraging theme.

The one uncompromising demand of this Gospel is belief
in Jesus as Son of God. To fail this demand is to die in sin (v.
21), because the one sin at the root of all sins is unbelief. It is
this issue which the Evangelist relentlessly pursues to the almost total neglect of the moral and ethical implications of
belief and unbelief. Unlike Matthew, there is no "Sermon on
the Mount" type material in this Gospel; unlike Paul there
are no catalogs of virtues and vices. The root of the matter
here is faith. There is no demand that one's confession of
faith be phrased one particular way: Son of God, Son of man,
Holy One of God, Savior of the world and other titles are
used. Neither is it required that one interpret one's Christology in metaphysical terms (of one essence with God) or biolog-
ical terms (born of a virgin). The one "right thing" to be
believed is that Jesus is from God and by his words and acts
he reveals God. To encounter Jesus is to encounter the truth
about God as creator, sustainer, and redeemer of the world
(1:1–18). If believing in Jesus does not inform, correct and
enlarge one's belief in God, then nothing has been achieved

except to give the impression that Jews believe in one God, Christians believe in two. In spite of its neglect, the central subject of the New Testament is God, and christological confessions should not stray from that. The Fourth Evangelist reminds us that we are not to use God to explain Jesus but rather listen to Jesus in order to understand God. For all the sharp tension between Jesus and "the Jews," it still is the case that the God who said "I am" to Moses (Exod 3:14) comes in the signs and words of Jesus as "I am" (v. 28).

Jesus and Abraham (8:31–59)

"Are you greater than our father Abraham?" (v. 38). In the debate between the synagogue and the church, the synagogue seemed to have the better of it. The synagogue had tradition, a rich and long tradition, and whoever speaks lightly of tradition fails to understand its many values for a community or an individual. Not even a radically new life could take from Paul his tradition as an Israelite (Rom 9:1–5). Tradition gives security, direction and identity. Tradition provides the narrative into which one is enrolled. Whoever cannot remember any farther back than birth is an orphan, dislodged in the world. Tradition provides an agenda for a community's life. Tradition offers some criteria by which to evaluate the fads and claims of each generation. Tradition brings the past into the present, making that past alive and available and nourishing. Tradition makes the faith of the ancestors available so that the community and its members may be sustained during dry and waterless days when its own experiences seem to contradict all the claims of faith. One does not relinquish tradition easily. Therefore, when Christians made claims about the centrality of Jesus Christ, it was normal and right for tradition to rise up and ask, "Are you greater than Jacob (chap. 4)? Are you greater than Moses (chap. 6)? Are you greater than Abraham (chap. 8)?"

But tradition can become perverted, becoming hardened and fixed, becoming imperialistic and demanding idolatrous allegiance. Rather than growing by being open to the present and the ways in which God continues to work, tradition can force the present to serve the past or be rejected. Had Jesus been content to fit comfortably into one of the sub-headings of the tradition, there would have been hardly a stir. But when he insisted upon starting a new chapter, the battle was on. However, it was not really a new chapter that Jesus had in mind. It was rather moving to the truth that lay prior to and superior to all historical expressions of it. Jesus speaks the word of God who called into existence a people. The paradigm for the people of God was Abraham, a pilgrim, a seeker, one who moved always toward the beckoning voice of God. But what has happened? Abraham is no longer a model of faith; Abraham is a badge. "We are children of Abraham" is the motto on the badge.

What Jesus does here is quite similar to what Paul did in arguments with legalists. Paul countered Mosaic legalism by moving 430 years earlier to Abraham and the covenant of faith. So here, Jesus is portrayed countering pride in the Abrahamic tradition with the prior claim of the eternal Word: "Before Abraham was, I am" (v. 58). Just as Paul insisted that not all of Israel are truly Israelites, so here, not all of Abraham are really of Abraham (vv. 37–40). In sharper terms, not all who claim to be of God are of God; not all who claim to be possessors of the truth have the truth; not all who claim to be free are free. The liberating truth (v. 32) is simply this: only God is absolute and final; all else is created of God and has its life in God and is sustained by being open to God's word and God's leading. To seek security in a tradition, a genealogy, a nation, or an institution is to believe the falsehood of idolatry. But to point out this error to those who embrace it is to become the object of hostility and bitter hatred. "So they took up stones to throw at him" (v. 59) is more than a line from the story of Jesus; it is a first century way of saying what has continually been the case. History demonstrates that anger is generated not alone by hearing one who is wrong but one who is right. Hearing the truth we painfully recognize puts us at war with ourselves, and when at war with ourselves we tend to make casualties of others, especially those who create the discomfort.

A brief word needs to be said about v. 48: "The Jews answered him, 'Are we not right in saying that you are a Samaritan and have a demon?' " It would be an error to treat this as the meaningless name calling of disputants who have

lost their tempers because they have lost the argument. Recall earlier comments to the effect that critics of Jesus sometimes voice the near truth, if not the truth. Such is the case
here. They call Jesus a Samaritan. He is not, and yet he was
among them, he abode with them, he had followers in Samaria. To those for whom it is inconceivable that anyone but a
Samaritan would live among Samaritans, this identification
of Jesus makes sense. In a way it is a compliment to Jesus
because it says that he ministered in close association, not
from a distance. Genuine ministry assumes some of the burden of the condition of those to whom one ministers, whether
they be Samaritans, the poor, sinners, social outcasts, the
rich, or the powerful. In fact, one cannot forgive another
without bearing in the public view something of the taint of
the one forgiven. Likewise with the charge that Jesus has a
demon. The critics thereby acknowledge a power in Jesus but
misunderstand its nature and source. He has the Spirit and it
is from God. But stand for a moment in the critics' place. To
have one come among them with power is intimidating and
disturbing. If the use of that power contradicts their values,
their customs and their positions, and threatens their world,
which are they more likely to say: he has the Spirit of God or
he has a demon? Now that we are standing in the critics'
place, we might ask ourselves if we have ever stood there
before.

Another Sabbath Healing—The Man Born Blind (9:1–41)

The story in this chapter comes as a surprise after 8:59
has informed the reader that Jesus moved out of public view
and hid from those who sought to kill him. Several theories
of mislocation and proposed relocation of chapter 9 relieve
this disjuncture but create new ones, besides lacking manu-
script evidence to support the theories. We have already noticed other places where the seams between units of material
are quite visible. But even so, there is a thematic continuity
between chapters 8 and 9. The dualism of light and darkness
continues not only in the words of Jesus (vv. 4–5) but also in
the sign act. Blindness and seeing are the response side of
darkness and light.

The reader will notice immediately in how many ways
this story is like the healing in chapter 5. Both are sign stories; that is, both are acts of Jesus that are revelatory and are
followed by discourses which elaborate upon that revelation.
Both healings occur on the sabbath which becomes a major
point of tension between Jesus and the Jews. In both cases
Jesus acts on his own initiative and not in response to a person's faith. In other words, both the lame and the blind came
to have faith in Jesus *as a result* of the healings; their faith is
not the cause for the healings. Those readers whose minds
and theologies are programmed for faith healings simply
must make adjustments appropriate to the theology of this
Gospel. (Those who try to force the Jesus of the Gospel into
the image of Jesus the faith healer found in the Synoptics
and in many subsequent traditions may be doing what the
Pharisees of this narrative are trying to do—define Jesus according to conclusions firmly fixed.) In both accounts there is
present the belief that physical illness is related to sin (5:14;
9:1), but in neither does such thinking dominate the message
aimed for the reader. And finally, in both stories the persons
who are healed suffer for the blessing received from Jesus
(5:10; 9:34). In one noticeable respect the narratives differ: in
chapter 9 the events and discussions which follow the healing all flow out of the sign act itself whereas in chapter 5,
subsequent discussions (vv. 19–47) are not directly related in
imagery or substance to the healing by the pool.

Because 9:1–41 is one unit, the preacher would do well
to treat the entire narrative in a message, and then, as conditions warrant, draw upon the main lines of the story for particular emphases on subsequent occasions. The account
unfolds as a drama, centering upon an act of Jesus which has
tremendous influence in the lives of many people. Scene one
(vv. 1–7) opens with Jesus and his disciples passing along
and observing a blind man. The disciples have no idea of doing anything for the man; they prefer a discussion of the possible causes of the man's condition. Look upon any scene of
human misery, ask Why? and the Kingdom of God turns into
a theological seminar. But not for Jesus who acts, says the
writer, in order to reveal the action of God. In a ritual of
healing not unlike that of other healers of the day, Jesus gave
sight to the blind man. Scene two (vv. 8–12) takes place in

the blind man's neighborhood. Friends and neighbors are watching and wondering and arguing. Is the man now seeing the same as the one born blind? It must be. It cannot be. They gather round the man, flooding him with questions. Who did it? How? Where is he? He told what he knew. In the third scene (vv. 13-17), the man has been hauled before the religious authorities. After all, this is a religious matter, being a miracle, and having been done on the sabbath it is also a criminal act. Heavy brows are lowered in listening to the man's story. The authorities are divided in the case: an act of God, say some; a criminal breach of the law, say others. In almost comic frustration, the clergy turn to the poor layman for a judgment to break the deadlock. His opinion? Jesus is a prophet (v. 17). Notice the growing courage and faith of the healed man. "The man called Jesus" (v. 11) is now Jesus the prophet. This witness is rejected and more evidence is sought.

In scene four (vv. 18–23), the healed man's parents stand frightened and intimidated before the authorities. It has been made clear that not only Jesus is on trial but also anyone who believes in him. In fact, to witness is to be punished. Under the threat of expulsion from the synagogue and hence loss of place and respect in their community, the parents distance themselves from Jesus and from their son. They prefer not to be involved.

Scene five (vv. 24–34) returns to scene three, but this time the session is more heated. If they can break the man under intense questioning and get him to denounce as a lawbreaker and sinner the one who healed him, that statement could be used to warn and discourage any others who might be inclined to follow Jesus. It is obvious now that the healed man is on trial. The charge? Being a disciple of Jesus. The man's faith and courage have now grown stronger even though he stands alone without the support of neighbors or parents. His response to the authorities is a model of testimony from experience ("I was blind, now I see") and from logic ("If Jesus were not of God how could he have opened my eyes?"). The interrogators have a difficult decision: believe the argument, the evidence and the witness or stay with their already fixed interpretation of the law. They decide for the latter and expel the man whom Jesus had healed.

In the closing scene (vv. 35–41), Jesus finds the man who has been expelled from the synagogue and reveals himself to him. The man whom we first met as born blind, who first was talking about the man Jesus, who came to believe Jesus was a prophet, now confesses his faith in Jesus as the Son of Man and worships him. And the drama ends with the pronouncement of Jesus that his presence in the world is a judgment. Those who cannot see now have light and can see. Those who say they already see and have no need for light are blinded by the light. The reader is not allowed simply to enjoy a wonderful story about Jesus who gives sight to the blind. Christ's coming creates a crisis and two kinds of results follow: light comes to those who acknowledge life is darkness without him; darkness comes to those who without him claim to see.

The preacher can learn from this chapter not only what to say but also how to say it. We have here an excellent example of dramatic form, and by that is meant that the reader is put in the position of a spectator observing the characters interact with one another. Except for the pronouncement in v. 39, the entire communication is indirect, with no evidence of the writer's being aware of the reader. In indirect communication the reader is not addressed directly but only as messages are received through identifying with the events or characters of the story. It is in identification that the power of such communication lies, as all who attend the theatre well know. The Fourth Evangelist who usually is very aware of the reader may also be aware here but has chosen to let the reader identify himself or herself in the story. In other words, where does one identify in this drama? Among the undecided neighbors, with the frightened and uninvolved parents, among the Bible-quoting critics of Jesus, with the disciples who wish to discuss the human condition, or is it with the healed man who has to pay dearly for the benefit of Jesus' blessing?

If anyone doubts that the form of this narrative is the indirect communication of dramatic action, notice that after the opening act of healing, Jesus leaves the stage and does not return until the closing scene in which he reveals himself and pronounces the judgment of his revelation. Because he is absent from the stage, no direct messages from Jesus can be given to the reader. In this regard this account is unique in the

Gospel. Who, then, is on stage in every scene? The man healed of blindness. He it is who tries to explain, who faces accusers, who suffers without family support, who confesses, who is expelled from the synagogue, who is a disciple of Jesus. The spotlight is on the follower of Jesus. Jesus appeared and opened the man's eyes; Jesus went away; Jesus came a second time to receive, confirm, and vindicate the disciple.

Can anyone miss, then, what the Evangelist is doing? The life of the disciple, the life of the church which lies between the coming of Jesus and the coming of Jesus, is being portrayed. The members of the Johannine community must have wept and prayed and laughed and hoped as they read this narrative, for the drama is their very own. Blessed by Jesus, to be sure, and able now to see the grace and truth of God through the word of Jesus, but since then what has life been for them? Explaining and arguing with old neighbors, suffering alienation from family members who do not believe, and being branded as heretics and expelled from the synagogue. But there is the firm hope of Jesus' final appearance in full revelation to confirm and to vindicate his disciples.

It would be regrettable if a preacher whose custom it was to hammer out direct exhortations Sunday after Sunday missed this opportunity to be instructed by this Evangelist in a different method of communicating the Gospel.

One final note: it is not at all certain, but quite possible that the re-appearance of Christ at the close of the drama was not solely for the purpose of confirming and vindicating his followers. There seems also to be a warning to his disciples in the words to the Pharisees: "If you were blind, you would have no guilt; but now that you say, 'We see,' your guilt remains" (v. 41). To become self-assured, to close the mind to any further word from God, to be the possessors of the final truth with no need to listen to prophets, to build institutions without the means and occasions of self-criticism would be to write into the script "disciples" instead of "Pharisees" and "church" instead of "synagogue."

Dispute over Leadership: The True Shepherd (10:1–21)

The commentaries will engage the student of this unit in a discussion of the problems that are quite evident when one reads the text. The problems are basically in three areas. The first has to do with the relation of 10:1–21 with chapter 9 and with 10:22–42. Since 10:1 has no temporal or geographical reference to lead into the material that follows, one would assume 10:1–21 continues the discussion of chapter 9. But one could argue that the radical shift in imagery, subject matter, and literary form make a strong case against this. However, since 9:35–41 concludes with Jesus addressing religious leaders, there is here a kind of continuity in that 10:1–21 deals with true and false leaders. But 10:22 specifies the time as the Feast of Dedication. Does that apply to vv. 1–21 as well as to vv. 22–42? If so, then 10:1–21 is not continuous with chapter 9; that is, if we assume that the last reference to time (Feast of Tabernacles) in 7:2 is to pertain until the end of chapter 9. With such uncertainties, it seems wisest not to tie the interpretation of 10:1–21 too closely to what precedes or follows. The unit has its own integrity and probably should be treated independently.

A second problem encountered in this passage is the introduction of figurative language. The modern reader may have understood this Gospel to contain figurative language throughout, "wine," "bread," "water" and "food" being but a few examples. However, from the writer's viewpoint, 10:6 is the first occasion for the use of the word *paroimia*, translated figure, image, analogy or even parable, to describe the discourse language of Jesus. It is obviously a deliberately chosen and very important word for this Evangelist by which he intends to convey a meaning the very opposite of "speaking plainly." For example, in 10:24, the Jews say to Jesus, "How long will you keep us in suspense? If you are the Christ, tell us *plainly*." In 16:25 Jesus says, "I have said this to you in *figures;* the hour is coming when I shall no longer speak to you in figures but tell you *plainly* of the Father." And in 16:29, "His disciples said 'Ah, now you are speaking *plainly*, not in any *figure!*'" Even in transliterated form the two Greek terms convey the play on words here *paroimia* (figure) and *parrasia* (plainly).

But much more than a play on words is at stake. The writer says that when Jesus spoke of shepherd, sheep, thief, robber and gatekeeper, his hearers did not understand (10:6). That Jesus' audiences did not understand him is not a new phenomenon; he was not understood when he spoke of building the temple in three days, or of being born from above, or of living water, or of food to eat not known to his disciples, or of manna from heaven, or of going to his Father, and countless other expressions. In each case, the language of Jesus was both revealing and concealing. To those who did not believe he was from God his words concealed; to those who believed (including the readers of the Gospel), Jesus' words revealed the truth. The revealing/concealing dynamic is at work in 10:1–21: the Jews did not understand but the readers of this Gospel do. But now that it is for the first time stated openly that Jesus spoke in figures, the question as to why he spoke with concealed meanings will not remain silent. There is a kind of secrecy operative here, and it presents no problem if the reason for not understanding lies totally in the listener's ear. However, if some measure of the responsibility is placed on the lips of the one speaking, then it gives us pause, especially if we have been taught all our lives that Jesus made everything plain and simple.

The water here is deep and the reader will recall earlier efforts to wade across. But let it be said here that no one should fault this Gospel for unnecessary obscurity and go fleeing to the Synoptics as though they were written at high noon. The irony, double meanings and figurative speech of this Evangelist are closely paralleled by the parables of the other Gospels. Recall Mark's comment about Jesus' use of parables. "And when he was alone, those who were about him with the twelve asked him concerning the parables. And he said to them, 'To you has been given the secret of the Kingdom of God, but for those outside everything is in parables' " (Mark 4:10–11). However one may account for it, the language of revelation is not obvious to all and sundry who happen to be passing by. Such transparency is vulgar. And yet neither is it contained only in the whispered secrets of the spiritually elite. In fact, what may strike a hearer as a figure at one time may be quite plain later. For example, to what are the disciples responding when they say in 16:29 that Jesus is no longer speaking in figures but is talking plainly? It is precisely what Jesus had been saying to them for several chapters! What has made the difference? The text offers the reader no clear explanation, but it seems safe to conclude

that understanding is as often a matter of character and trust
as it is intelligence. There is much here for the preacher to
ponder, and much to learn from the ways the Bible itself
preaches. Of first importance is the skill to use language in
such a way as to have a method of communicating congenial
to the message itself.

The third problem in our text is that of its internal unity.
This is not an issue among scholars of only peripheral concern to the preacher. On the contrary, compressed within
10:1–21, and especially within vv. 1–16 are so many images
and lines of thought that no sermon could embrace them all.
A sermon text should be a unit with a governing theme. What
are the discernible units within 10:1–21? Although the opinion is by no means unanimous, the preacher could well accept, for purposes of clarity and unit of presentations, the
following divisions of vv. 1–21:

10:1–6—Even though some scholars regard vv. 1–3a as
one figure and vv. 3b–6 another, there is a sufficiently visible
center to vv. 1–6 so as to treat it as a unit.

10:7–10—Here again, some analysts regard vv. 7–8 as
one commentary on vv. 1–5 and vv. 9–10 as another. That
these verses are commentary on vv. 1–5 is quite possible. Recall again Mark 4:1–20 in which a parable is followed by a
commentary on the parable, with the explanation much
more difficult to understand than the original story.

10:11–18—This unit is less complex, leaving the image of
thief, robber, door, shepherd and gatekeeper, and focusing
upon the single contrast between a shepherd and a hireling.

10:19–21—The familiar summary of mixed responses to
Jesus' discourse.

In vv. 1–6 the principal thought has to do with how one
approaches the flock with the contrasting figures of the shepherd and the thieves and robbers. The shepherd comes naturally to the flock, acting in trust and loving care. The
relationship between shepherd and sheep was a familiar one
in that culture and so marked by a special closeness as to
provide the Old Testament with images of God's care for
Israel (Isa 40:11; Ps 23) and the New Testament with images
of Christ's love for the lost and helpless (Luke 15:3–7; Mark
6:34). But who were the thieves and bandits? If the recipients
of this Gospel read it historically, they probably thought of

those leaders among the Jews who used their positions and
political connections with the Herods and Rome to their own
profit and security. Since the Maccabeans the people had suffered under many such local tyrants. To them the common
people were a flock of sheep valued as so much flesh and
fleece. "Thieves and bandits" could also describe some insur-
rectionists, rebel leaders and self-proclaimed messiahs who
became as oppressive as the oppressors they would over-
throw. But it is most likely that the Johannine community
did not look solely to history to identify those who come
through the back doors and windows of the church, claiming
to be apostles and prophets, promising leadership, mouthing
scripture and invoking the Holy Spirit. The entire New Testament and other early Christian literature warned the
churches of those who line their stomachs and their purses,
leaving behind a divided, confused, hurt and discouraged
flock. And twenty centuries later the church continues to be
victimized by thieves and robbers who find the people of God
an easy mark. Such violations will continue whenever and
wherever the church does not develop criteria by which to
discern the thief in the sheepfold.

In vv. 7–10 the governing image is that of Christ as the
door. The image functions both as polemic and as promise;
as polemic in relation to those false leaders whose work is
destructive and as promise for the Christian community.
Whatever the types of persons or groups who sought to gain
access to the Johannine flock, whether from synagogue, Baptist sect, or heretical Christian circles, the key to such access
was Christ. Whether Christ as door meant belief in him as
Son of God or following his model of caring ministry, or
both, the point is that Christ served as the canon by which to
measure and evaluate Christian ministry. The Shepherd is
the door to shepherding, and the flock that knows the Shepherd can recognize his voice in the teaching, preaching and
pastoring of those who are his shepherds.

In relation to the church membership, Christ as door is a
promise of both security ("will be saved") and freedom ("will
go in and out and find pasture"). No doubt the description of
Christ's relation to the church here is drawn from the ap-
pointment of Joshua (Jesus) as leader of Israel. "Moses said
to the Lord, 'Let the Lord, the God of the spirits of all flesh,

appoint a man over the congregation, who shall go out before
them and come in before them, who shall lead them out and
bring them in; that the congregation of the Lord may not be
as sheep which have no shepherd'" (Num 27:15–17). The
writer knows, of course, as well as we do that it is one thing
to say that Jesus Christ is the real leader of the church but
quite another to say how, in the absence of Christ as the
Johannine and subsequent churches experienced it, this leadership manifests itself. How is the unity of Christ and his
church to be effected and confirmed? To that matter the farewell discourses (chaps. 14-16) and prayer (chap. 17) will attend. However, it should be said now that the close
relationship of Christ and his followers, here described in the
image of the shepherd and his sheep and later in the image of
the vine and the branches (15:1–11), is not solely an elusively
mystical one. It is a union in the word which Christ has revealed, and that word has double confirmation: the unbroken tradition of a witness to what Christ said and did (19:35;
21:24), and the witness of the Holy Spirit (14:25–26; 15:26;
16:13–14). Any voice calling to the flock that departs from
this word is the voice of a stranger.

In vv. 11–18 the work of Jesus as the model shepherd is
presented in the ultimate act of caring, the giving of one's
life. This act of love stands out all the more impressively
against the dark backdrop of the hirelings who, upon the
slightest threat of danger, abandon the sheep and run. If
there is an Old Testament background to the shepherd's giving his life for the sheep, it may be the account of David risk-
ing his life against bear and lion in behalf of the sheep (1
Sam 17:34–35). In later times this model of Christ as shepherd served as the ground for exhorting pastors to give themselves in the care of the flock, whether the danger was the
insinuating entrance of false teachers (Acts 20:28–30) or open
persecution (1 Pet 5:1–2). When one recalls the pressures and
dangers confronting the church addressed by this Gospel
(15:18–25; 16:1–4), the model of Jesus as the pastor who will
stay with the flock, whatever the cost, is a most appropriate
one, as is the warning about pastors-for-pay who cut and run
when problems pile up. In fact, there has never been a time
when the images were not appropriate, and there has never
been a time when there were not pastors who remembered.

Before Roman sword or Nazi boot, burning crosses or threat
of exile, economic reversal or police brutality, these have refused to abandon the flock. And then there are the hirelings.

Two notes in closing. One concerns the identification of
the other sheep not of this fold (v. 16). The first thought is of
the Gentile mission, a concern certainly underscored elsewhere in this Gospel (11:52; 12:19–24). But it is possible to
understand "other sheep" as those subsequent generations of
Christians who are in no way excluded or secondary to the
original circle. These, too, receive this writer's attention
(17:20; 20:29). A sermon moving in either direction would
not violate the concerns and sympathies of this Evangelist.
The second note is simply a reminder to the reader that vv.
17–18 are fully consistent with the portrait of Christ drawn
throughout the Gospel. Even though one may be accustomed
to reading that *God* raised Jesus from the dead (Acts 2:24;
Rom 4:24; Eph. 1:20 and elsewhere), the Christ of the Fourth
Gospel is one with the Father and the will or power of the
one is the will or power of the other. As in his ministry, so in
his death and resurrection, Christ is in control.

At the Feast of Dedication: Tension Mounts, Jesus Withdraws (10:22–42)

The preacher may choose not to tarry long in 10:22–42.
This is not to say that the material is unimportant; on the
contrary, the dispute between Jesus and the Jews here concerns the person of Jesus and this is the heart of this Gospel.
But the point, the dispute, has been aired repeatedly before.
In fact, 10:22–42 is so similar to the events and conversations
located at the time of the Feast of Tabernacles that some
commentators use the word "duplicates" in referring to the
verses before us. Jesus is in Jerusalem in the precincts of the
temple, as before. Jesus is pressed to declare openly if he is
the Christ and he refuses on the grounds that they would not
believe him if he did, as before. Jesus declares he and the Father are one and the Jews attempt to stone him, as before.
Jesus is charged with blasphemy which, while not stated directly, has been clearly implied, as early as 5:18. Jesus an-
swers their charges from their own Bible, as he has done
before. Again, they try unsuccessfully to arrest Jesus, as
before. And again Jesus retreats, this time to the old scenes of

John the Baptist's first ministry. There crowds gather about
Jesus, and the echo of John's witness, confirmed now by the
signs which Jesus did, moves them to faith. It has long since
become familiar to hear the writer say "many believed,"
only to move into the next story and meet unbelief and
hostility.

Except for the conclusion in vv. 40–42, this unit consists
of parallel accounts in vv. 22–31 and vv. 32–39. The first centers in the question of whether Jesus is the Messiah. As always Jesus does not give a direct answer but lets his works
argue his case (recall Jesus' response to John the Baptist
when John asked for a direct answer, Matt 11:2–5). Jesus insists that it is not more evidence they need but a different
relationship to God. As Chrysostom expressed it, they do not
follow Jesus, not because he is not a shepherd but because
they are not sheep. Upon Jesus' claiming oneness with the
Father they attempt to stone him, which ends the first
account.

The second account is essentially the same except the
question is not whether Jesus is the Messiah but whether he
claims to be God. The line of argument Jesus used to counter
his opponents is most difficult to follow and the commentaries will take the reader through the various possibilities. He
quotes Ps 82:6 which is a statement God makes to the divine
council in heaven. In the council are the messengers, admin-
istrators, and judges who are assigned the responsibility of
seeing that God's creatures on earth are provided for and
that justice is done. Apparently through these heavenly be-
ings revelations as at Sinai occur. These agents of God are
called "gods" and "sons of the Most High." Apparently,
Jesus' point is that if these messengers of the word are called
gods, and in their own Bibles, why charge with blasphemy
the one who *is* the Word and who says he is the Son of God?
Of course, the argument falls on deaf ears and the account
ends with an attempt to arrest Jesus.

All this, of course, sounds very familiar by now, but also
just as strange as when it began to occur in chapter 5. What
is to be made of it? Three brief comments seem to be in
order.

One, we are listening in on the kinds of argument that
took place between the church and synagogue. Obviously

these debates were based on presuppositions not necessarily ours: a certain relationship between church and synagogue; tenets of Jewish theology and messianism; rabbinic methods of interpreting and arguing Scripture; and certain defini-tions of terms such as Son of God. It would not be meaning-ful, therefore, to transform to a modern Gentile Christian congregation the intricacies of these disputes and declare Jesus the winner. That would be an exercise in chauvinistic triumphalism. But it would be and is appropriate to ask whether the church today believes there is enough at stake to tangle with the current structure of opposition to the Gospel, structures that are economic, political and radical, as well as personal and moral.

Two, here and elsewhere in this Gospel, the constant ap-peal for proof of the Christian message is to "the works." The "works" refer in the first instance to the ministry of Jesus, but since Jesus commissioned the church to do what he did and even more (14:12), neither the Johannine nor the modern church could persuasively make its case by appealing solely to the wonderful things Jesus did back then. It remains the burden to continue the line of argument attributed here to Jesus, and to say to all critics and detractors: "If you do not believe our words, believe the works that we do." The ques-tion is, would this be a convincing argument?

Third and finally, consider the importance of the Feast of Dedication as the time and place of these disputes. This feast is the Feast of Hannukah, observed in the winter (v. 22), near the time of the Christian celebration of Christmas. Hannukah commemorated the victory of the Maccabeans over the Syri-ans, the recovery of the temple and particularly the consecra-tion of the altar which had been profaned by the Syrians (these events occurred about 160 B.C.).

Earlier we called attention to the ministry and words of Jesus on other festival days: Sabbath, Passover, and Tabernacles. In each case, the Evangelist has developed a view of Jesus as the replacement of the festival. Now at the Feast of Dedication, Jesus declares himself the one consecrat-ed or dedicated by the Father (v. 36). He is the tabernacle where God's glory resides (1:14); he is the temple of God to be raised again in three days (2:19–21); now he is the altar, consecrated of God and the replacement of the entire sacrificial system. And it is inescapable that attention to the altar of sacrifice would turn the reader to thoughts of Jesus' approaching death. In this way the Evangelist prepares us for that series of events which prophesy that death.

The Witness of Events Which Prophesy Jesus' Death
(John 11:1—12:50)

With these two chapters the record of Jesus' public ministry comes to a close. To speak of the events narrated here as prophetic of Jesus' death is appropriate, but such a designation can be misleading. The subject of the death of Jesus surfaced as early as 2:19 and re-appeared with some frequency thereafter. But with every threat of mob action or of attempts at arrest, the reader was told that "the hour had not yet come." In these two chapters, however, talk of death permeates each story and the reader experiences the dramatic intensification which signals that "the hour has come."·

Jesus Gives Life to Lazarus (11:1–44)

The commentaries will discuss at length the question of whether the story of raising Lazarus came from a source known also to Luke. With this discussion the preacher will want to become familiar, if for no other reason than to keep the account before us distinct and clear of those blurrings which occur when two writers treat the same or similar subject matter. John 11:1–44 seems to come in contact with the Gospel of Luke, or with material known to Luke, at several points. There is the common knowledge of the sisters Martha and Mary (Luke 10:38–42) along with very similar characterizations of the two. There is also the common use of the name Lazarus, although in Luke he appears as a poor beggar in a story Jesus told (16:19–31). The story is often called a parable, but in parables proper names are not used to refer to the characters. One could dismiss the common use of the name Lazarus as coincidental were it not for the fact that in both John 11 and Luke 16 Lazarus is involved in the matter of death and resurrection. And a third point at which these two Gospels seem to touch is in the portrayal of Jesus weeping (John 11:35; Luke 19:41). However, as we shall see, the tears of Jesus in the text before us, unlike Luke, are quite enigmatic in both cause and meaning.

But whatever the source of this story and whatever its
function in that source, for this Evangelist the raising of Lazarus is a sign story. To say it is a sign is to say about it at
least two things: first, Jesus will act according to his own
time and not according to any pressures put upon him,
friendly or unfriendly. This has been made clear in Jesus' re-
marks to his mother (chap. 2), to the crowd (chap. 6), to his
brothers (chap. 7) and to his disciples (chap. 9). The reader
should not be disturbed, therefore, by Jesus' response to the
urgent message from his friends: he stayed two days longer
where he was (v. 6). In this Gospel, the actions of Jesus are
"from above" and therefore transcend the contingencies of
the particular circumstances of his own time and place in
history. Second, to say this story is a sign is to say that its
primary function is revelation. By means of the ministry of
Jesus, some truth about what the glory (presence) of God in
the world really means is made known. Since Jesus Christ is
the one in whom the grace and truth of God are made flesh,
in the story that follows the reader is invited to see the One
whom no one has ever seen (1:18).

Having said that the understanding of this narrative depends upon seeing it as a sign and, therefore, like the other
signs in the Gospel, it must also be said that understanding
the Lazarus story depends upon seeing at least three major
respects in which this account differs from preceding ones.
One difference lies in the statement of the purpose of the
sign, which is not only for the glory of God but "that the Son
of God may be glorified by means of it" (v. 4). This is to say
that by means of the sign act involving Lazarus, or stated
more strongly, the purpose of what Jesus does involving Laz-

arus is the glorifying of the Son. In this Gospel, the glorifying
of the Son is a reference to the Son's return to the Father. The
means of that return is the cross and, therefore, to be lifted
up on the cross is to be lifted up to God's presence. "To glorify the Son" is, then, a way of speaking of the death, resurrection and ascension of Jesus Christ (12:23–26, 32). The reader
is therefore alerted at the outset that the story about to unfold has as its center not a family crisis in Bethany but the
crisis of the world, and what will transpire is not simply re-
suscitating a corpse but giving life to the world. In other
words, the subject is not the death and resurrection of Laza-

rus but the death and resurrection of Jesus. By so understanding it, the story is relieved of those painfully nagging
questions that will not go away if the text is treated as something Jesus did to help a bereaved family. For example, if
Jesus loved them, why did he not go running when he heard
of Lazarus' illness? We would have. Or again, are we to conclude that if you are Jesus' friend your deceased relative is
returned to you, but if not, too bad? Or again, assuming Lazarus will die again, are the sisters really helped by being put
in the position of having two periods of grief and paying for
two funerals? And on and on and on the questions flow, unless one handles the story as the Evangelist does, and that is
as a sign which points beyond itself to a truth about Jesus
Christ. That truth, as we shall see, is stated to Martha (vv.
25–26).

Granted, this Gospel leaves many questions unanswered
by treating events as signs. Our historical curiosity prefers
that the camera remain on the event long enough for our
questions about what really happened to be satisfied. But all
we have is the text, and to focus upon the event and to manu-
facture factual details would be to join all those in the Gospel
who have no eye or ear for the message but who have huge
appetite for more signs. Of course, there are times when ministers would prefer that this be a simple story of Jesus' compassion, upon which could be built funeral sermons about
Jesus in the cemetery. But is not more gained than lost if the
minister says what the writer says: apart from trust in God
the world is a cemetery, but into the world God has sent in
Jesus Christ the offer of resurrection, the opportunity to pass
from death to life. Just as the crowds wanted bread and he
offered Bread, so here the sisters want their brother returned
and Jesus acts to restore the world to life.

To act in this larger life-giving way means Jesus must
move to his own death, and so he does. His disciples are quite
aware that a return to Bethany and to Judea is a turn toward
the death which they had, by retreating and hiding, thus far
avoided. True to form, they misunderstand when Jesus says
Lazarus is asleep (vv. 11–13), but lack of understanding does
not mean lack of loyalty. "Let us also go, that we may die
with him" (v. 16.)

A second major difference between this and previous

signs is that the sign act itself comes at the end rather than
at the beginning of the account. The pattern up to this point
in the Gospel is fairly consistent: the sign followed by a discourse or dispute. But here the narrative follows the princi-
ple of end stress, the sign coming after the gradual
heightening of dramatic tension. Word comes of Lazarus' illness; to go to Bethany is to return to the danger zone; Jesus
delays; Jesus returns, followed by frightened but loyal disciples; Martha meets Jesus, tells him he is too late, chides him
and yet trusts him; Mary comes to Jesus and in an emotion-
filled scene Jesus weeps; Jesus goes to the tomb, followed by
the reluctant sisters and a questioning crowd; Jesus orders
the stone removed; Jesus prays and then screams at Lazarus
to come out; Lazarus emerges, wrapped in grave cloth; Jesus
commands some persons nearby to unwrap Lazarus and let
him go. The deed is done and as surely as Lazarus left the
tomb, Jesus must enter it, for Jesus himself said it, one cannot give life unless one dies (12:24).

A word to the preacher: while this story contains many
verses sufficiently meaningful to be sermon texts, it would be
a mistake to treat any of the narrative without re-telling the
whole of it, and in the dramatic sequences as they stand in
the text. Too many sermons take excerpts from the account
assuming that the full story is familiar. For many hearers
this is not the case, but even if it were, that is hardly an adequate reason not to tell it in full. Two groups of people are
moved by a well-told story of life and death: those who have
not heard it and those who have.

The third and final major difference between this sign
and previous ones is the level and intensity of opposition
which it draws. There had been earlier efforts to stone Jesus
or to arrest Jesus, but now in the chief seats of power brows
are lowered over the gravity of the situation. The Jewish
supreme court, the Sanhedrin, is called into session. The
leaders are concerned that the increasing size of Jesus' following poses a threat to domestic tranquility. The Romans
may sense civil unrest, move in with soldiers, remove the
Jewish leadership and declare martial law. The chief priest
Caiaphas is clear in his judgment: Jesus must die. There remains undetermined only the scheme by which to do it (vv.
45–53). While the description of the dark aftermath lies

outside the account of the sign itself and will receive separate
treatment later, it needs at least this brief attention now in
order to see how the statement of Jesus concerning the purpose of the sign is being fulfilled: "It is for the glory of God,
so that the Son of God may be glorified by means of it" (v. 4).

Two matters remain for consideration: the portrait of
Jesus as troubled and upset, and the word of Jesus to Martha
concerning the resurrection and life eternal. The description
of Jesus as "deeply moved in spirit and troubled" (v. 33),
weeping (v. 35) and "deeply moved again" (v. 38) would not
draw special attention were it in any Gospel other than this,
but here it surprises the reader. Many, of course, have wel-
comed these lines, relieved that the Son from above, eternal
and one with God, all knowing and completely in charge of
every situation, is not without human emotion. But little if
any of this dimension of the Word made flesh has been visible up to this point. Why now? Because of grief for his friend?
Perhaps, but that hardly seems adequate given Jesus' delib-
erate delays and the fact that this is the interpretation given
by "the Jews" (v. 36) who are in this Gospel consistently
wrong. Does Jesus weep over the unbelief of those about him,
as he did in Luke 19:41–44? Perhaps, but how does this unbelief differ from that encountered every other day of his ministry? Do we have here the Fourth Evangelist's description of
Jesus' Gethsemane? Perhaps; there certainly is no agony in
the garden the night of the arrest (18:1–11), so it may be that
the agony is re-located here. It makes a kind of sense to understand vv. 28–44 in view of the fact that Jesus had said this
event would eventuate in his own death. In fact, one cannot
read the account and continue to think of Lazarus; one thinks
of Jesus. Notice: Jesus troubled and weeping; a tomb not far
from Jerusalem; the tomb is a cave with a large stone cover-
ing the opening; the stone is rolled away; Jesus cries with a
loud voice; the grave cloth. Sounds familiar, even if the sequence is not.

However the preacher may interpret the portrait of Jesus
here, two lines of thought are unavoidably clear and of primary importance. One, Jesus submits to the same demand
given to those called to follow him. Even though he is Lord,
he is not exempt from the conditions placed upon us all. Notice that the tears of Jesus came immediately after he was

told, "Lord, come and see" (v. 34). The expression "come and
see," which is the formula for calling disciples, is now said to
Jesus. He hears his own words to others now spoken to him.
The best commentary on the experience is in 12:27: "Now is
my soul troubled. And what shall I say, 'Father, save me from
this hour'?" In other words, is the leader to be exempt from
the demands and discipline required of followers? No. Regardless of the policies by which other institutions operate,
in the church there is no primrose path for the shepherd and
thorny road for the flock. Two, the passage before us is a vivid reminder that even in this unusual Gospel, the Christian
faith is not otherworldly. With all the attention upon the One
from heaven, the writer has given details of geography and
place; with all the attention upon the eternal, the writer has
marked days and hours; with all the attention upon the
Word, the writer anchors it to the earth with six words: "the
Word became flesh" and "Jesus wept."

The other matter remaining for comment is the word
to Martha, which is probably the central message of the
narrative. She had expressed to Jesus her faith in a resurrection at the last day (v. 24), a faith shared by members
of the Pharisee party. As a correction to her faith, Jesus
declares that he is the eschatological event, he is the point
where death ends and life begins, he makes eternity now,
he provides to all who believe life on both sides of the
grave. Martha, like the mother of Jesus at Cana, believed
Jesus was able to do something although she did not know
what (v. 22). And, of course, she has no idea the price
Jesus will pay to give life to Lazarus and to the world.
Even so, through the encounter with Jesus in this critical
moment, her faith is deepened and enlarged to the point
she is able to confess that Jesus is the Christ, the Son of
God (v. 27). Since this is the very same confession which
this Gospel was written to generate in the readers (20:31),
it is correct to assume such faith whenever, wherever, and
by whomever confessed, lays hold to life no less abundant
and eternal than that which is dramatically presented
here. It is regrettable that many Christians do not know
this, because they have heard Jesus' words, "I am the resurrection and the life," used to support a faith no larger
than that of Martha before she heard these words. They do

not know that Jesus offers more than a confirmation of the old comfortless belief in a resurrection at the last day.

Jesus Is Condemned to Die (11:45–57)

Attention was drawn earlier to this section, but some comments are in order for the sake of the sermon. This passage provides the preacher as clear an example as the Gospel contains of a view of life from two perspectives. One perspective is from ground level in which events are described as experienced by participants, and the other is that of the reader, looking at events through the theology of the Evangelist.

On the one level, life is here portrayed as ugly and vicious, and as realistic as could be imagined. Jesus has just given life, and those in power who maintain control over others by the threat of death are disturbed. The drama takes place on a small stage because these are only puppet rulers, in office by the permission of the great power, Rome. They meet with one item on the agenda: not Jesus, not Lazarus, not life, but law and order. In other words, how can we keep our positions. The greater power (Rome) must not be disturbed or we may all be thrown out. Law and order means death to the One who opposes death, the One who opens tombs and sends shouts of life and freedom down the grim and empty hallways of our institutions. But it is not to be bare, naked, undisguised death for him. No, his death shall be a wise and expedient act in the service of peace, for the good of the people and the nation. Tragic, yes; regrettable, of course, but in the long run, it is better for us all this way. In a beautiful stroke of sarcasm, the Evangelist calls Caiaphas "high priest that year" (vv. 49, 51). In Jewish tradition the high priest was such for life, but now, under Rome, a breath could make or unmake a high priest. Those who sit so uneasily place political expedience above the word of God. He was not God's man; he was not even his own man; he was Rome's man. And so Caiaphas and the court decide, and the "wanted" posters are put in place: "Anyone having information as to the whereabouts of this man. . . ."

On the other level, the same scene is part of a drama so large the characters have no idea of the real parts they play. "One man must die for the people," said the high priest, not realizing the higher truth of his political opinion (vv. 49–52).

Not only the Jews but the whole world would be beneficiary in that death. "They took counsel how to put him to death" (v. 53), not knowing that they still had to wait upon Jesus' initiative, for he would lay down his life; no one would take it from him. They put word out on the street that they were looking for Jesus, not knowing that in a few days he would enter the city in a parade down Main Street. In the meantime, the Passover crowd gathers, whispering in corners and under the stairs, wagering whether or not Jesus would come for the feast.

Now what does the preacher do with this? One thing the preacher does *not* do, and that is to view this and all other scenes *only* from the second level. To do so is to be arrogant, peering over the bannister of spirituality down upon the pitiful dramas of human history, forgetting that "God so loved the *world*." To do so is to be totally unrealistic and irresponsible, for all of us live in that world, share in its pains and joys, and join in both its good and demonic uses of power. This truth can never be avoided by those who believe God creates, sustains, and redeems the world. But having said that, the preacher will not, as this Evangelist did not, let the church see itself solely as victim in such a world. Because the church believes finally in the sovereignty of God, it sees the larger drama, set on a stage bigger than Jerusalem, where there is a Council beyond the council and a Power that is not Rome. In this faith, the church has not been content to let its final word about the fate of Jesus be "murder" or "execution," or even "tragedy." Rather the church says, "God sent his Son," "Jesus gave his life," "Christ died for us." From one level one looks upon this scene and sees a lamb bleeding, a victim of injustice, fear, and violence. From another level one sees a lamb bleeding, but seated on a throne (Rev 5:9–14).

Jesus Is Anointed for Burial (12:1–8)

The first task of the interpreter of this passage is to keep this text in view rather than a composite of this and the similar accounts in the Synoptics (Mark 14:3–9; Matt 26:6–13; Luke 7:36–39). In spite of important differences among them, the common elements argue persuasively for a common source, oral or written. But here again, the preacher is to be

informed not distracted nor distracting in grappling with
John 12:1–8. The story as told by this Evangelist has its own
message.

The second task of the interpreter is to hear that
message. And what is it? The heart of the story is the approaching death of Jesus. All sub-plots in 12:1–8 must, therefore, relate to this governing theme and not provide side trips
for the preacher. Into one dark pattern all threads are beautifully woven. The scene is Bethany where there waits a now
available cave tomb; the time is Passover which in this Gospel is death time; at the table is Lazarus whose life cost Jesus
his (11:4); and there is the anointing which Jesus says is for
his burial. Notice also how the writer introduces into this
pleasant circle of Jesus and friends the dark intruder Judas
who is, by the time of this Gospel, viewed not only as traitor
but as thief. And there is that now familiar Johannine touch
to the story in the act of Mary. Out of love and gratitude she
enlarges an act of hospitality into a drama of devotion and
beauty. For the rest of her life she must have experienced
both grief and joy; grief that she who had so recently prepared her brother's corpse was now unwittingly anointing
her friend for burial, joy that she has this small part in
Christ's redeeming act. But "unwittingly" is the word; just
as Caiaphas unwittingly prophesied Jesus' death as a saving
act, so Mary's act of gratitude has a deeper meaning in the
grander purpose of God. All our acts and words have meanings and effects by no means limited to what we intend at the
time.

Whether or not it evolves into a sermon, the act of Mary
will both bless and plague the mind of the minister, for what
she did will be duplicated a thousand times over in the sin-
cere if often ill-advised expressions of devotion and gratitude
to Christ by church members. Three hundred poinsettias fill
the chancel at Christmas, five hundred lilies surround the
cross at Easter. Then there is the gift of sterling communion
ware, the memorial chimes, the stained-glass window. "In
gratitude," says the donor; "a sinful waste," says not only
Judas, but everyone who has seen hollow eyes over a tin cup
or heard the whimpering of a hungry child. Common sense
says we should plant onions, not roses, and yet a check of the
shopping list, even of the poor, will reveal that among pota-

toes, beans and pork will be flowers and perfume. And to all
this what shall the minister say?

Jesus Enters Jerusalem (12:9–19)

It may be a surprise to some that the account of Jesus'
entry into Jerusalem is so subdued in this Gospel which
seems to exalt or elevate Jesus to a degree beyond the Synoptics. Not only is the record briefer than that of Mark, but the
text of Zech 9:9, which is central to the church's understanding of the event, is summarized rather than quoted (either
from the Hebrew or Greek). However, the surprise subsides
upon careful reading and reflection. While it is true that this
Gospel contains what is commonly called a "high Christology," the status of Christ in no way depends on the public or
upon general adoration. Only once is he worshipped and
then by only one person (9:38). On the contrary, Jesus retreats from public efforts to make him king (6:15). Jesus is
Lord and King by virtue of who he is, totally apart from public praise. Faith does not make him who he is; faith recog-
nizes who he is. Careful reading of this Gospel's telling of the
event makes it clear that this is, like the two preceding, a
Lazarus story. It was the raising of Lazarus that gathered the
crowd and the reader is told four times that these people are
there because of the sign at Bethany and that the witnessing
to Jesus centers in the raising of Lazarus. In addition, the
death threatened against Jesus is now broadened to include
Lazarus also (vv. 10–11). And so, even over the shouting and
praise of the "triumphal entry" hangs the shadow of 11:4:
"so that the Son of God may be glorified by means of it."

No one understands all of this, of course; that is, no one
but the reader. The crowd shouts its praise because a man
has been called out of the tomb, unaware that Jesus' hour
has come to enter the tomb. Even the disciples, says the writer, did not understand until afterwards the meaning of Zech
9:9 or of this occasion (v. 16). Surely the members of the
Johannine church were encouraged to realize that they were
in a position to understand what the disciples present for the
event did not. And all of us should pause again to be blessed
by the thought that distance from a person or an event is not
always a negative factor. Distance can sharpen rather than
blur understanding, and hence increase faith and participa-

tion. In their ignorance, however, the critics and opponents
of Jesus utter the most profound truths about what was happening that day, and all the more remarkable since they did
not realize what they were saying (the preacher may wish to
develop a mini-series of sermons on truths from the lips of
those who did not know what they said). They acknowledge
the enormity of the occasion and their own impotence in relation to what is taking place: "You see that you can do nothing" (v. 19).

One last word about Lazarus, or rather about all to
whom Jesus has given new life. The church which reads this
Gospel has already learned that discipleship is not without
price. The lame man who was healed was arrested for sab-
bath-breaking (chap. 5); the blind man who received sight
was expelled from the synagogue because he had become a
disciple of Jesus (chap. 9). And now Lazarus, who had been
called out of death into life, must bear the reproach, the
threat and the death of his Lord. The servant is not greater
than the master. Even after all these years, it is not inappropriate to ask would-be disciples, "Do you realize what you
are doing?"

Jesus Announces the Hour Has Come (12:20–50)

"The hour has come for the Son of Man to be glorified"
(v. 23). This announcement is prompted by the coming of the
Greeks to see Jesus, which in turn was prompted by the
statement of the Pharisees, "the world has gone after him"
(v. 19), and altogether the narrative fulfills 11:52: "and not
for the nation only, but to gather into one the children of God
who are scattered abroad." The Greeks mentioned here are
probably Greeks who practice Judaism. Their coming to
Jesus through Philip and Andrew may be understood historically by the fact of the Greek names of these disciples and
their background in Galilee, which put them closer to the
Gentiles than would a Judean background. Understood eccle-
siastically, Philip and Andrew may represent an apostolic
mission to the Gentiles.

The central question, however, is this: What is there in
the request of the Greeks that prompts Jesus' announcement? The answer does not lie in a theory of the atoning
death of Jesus, such theories finding little nourishment in

this Gospel. The answer lies in the matter of presence, of availability. The Word in flesh was available to those who were in that place, at that time. Glorified, Christ is present to his people in all nations, in all generations. The Johannine church, being of another time and place, needed very much to hear this. And so do we, for without some clear doctrine of the continuing and unlimited presence of Christ, the church cannot live. No community of faith can long survive on the thin diet of fond memories of a Camelot, that marvelous time and place when he was here, a time and place that is no more. In such a case, faith would give way to resentment toward a God who was quite active long ago but who has done nothing within our lifetime. To expand upon the theme of Christ's continuing presence in the church will be the burden of the farewell speeches (chaps. 14–16), and so we will return to the matter soon.

As a kind of commentary upon his glorification, Jesus develops a three-stage line of thought. One, there is a law of nature that death is essential for the increase of life (v. 24). Two, there is a law of discipleship that death is the pre-condition of full life (v. 25). Third, does the law of nature and of discipleship apply to the Lord of nature and Master of disciples (v. 27)? And the answer is Yes. Some commentators on this passage have called it a "correction" of the Synoptic Gethsemane. Rather than "let this cup pass" Jesus says, "Exempt me? Never!" Instead of a cry of dereliction, Jesus prays and heaven voices confirmation (v. 28). And even though Jesus says his soul is troubled (v. 27), he is not in the throes of a struggle and has no need for a voice from heaven (v. 30).

Whether or not a "correction" of any kind is intended, the fact remains that there are no clouds in the Johannine sky. The transition in mood from the talk of foreboding death in preceding paragraphs could be compared to the break in a patient's fever. Although death for Jesus lies ahead, in a sense it now lies behind him. Some of us have known persons who have by faith come to such a point that they live and talk as those for whom death is a past experience. They have genuinely passed out of death into life.

The mood shifts at the point of heaven's confirmation of Jesus' embrace of the cross as the will of God. Of course, not all heard the voice; some thought an angel spoke while others said it thundered (v. 29). Not only the Gospel but experience itself has taught us not to be puzzled nor surprised by this. Not even those who are fully persuaded that they were called to ministry can testify that the voice of God was loud enough for the whole family to hear. With the "lifting up" (v. 32) of Jesus upon the cross and to God's presence as the subject, the remainder of the chapter speaks of Jesus' death in two ways. It is judgment in the sense that light is judgment upon those preferring darkness, and it is judgment in the sense that life is judgment upon those who prefer death. The death of Jesus is also spoken of as victory. It is a victory over the ruler of this world (v. 31), the powers of evil which separate creation from Creator and then persuade creation that darkness and death are simply "the way it is down here." It is a victory also in the sense that through the presence of Christ in word and in the Holy Spirit, persons of all nations and all times will be drawn again to God (v. 32).

The Evangelist brings to a close the narrative of Jesus' public ministry with two strong paragraphs. The first, 12:37–43, is a word of judgment upon the Jews. "Though he had done so many signs before them, yet they did not believe in him" (v. 37). From the time the followers of Jesus first began to experience the growth of hostile distance from the synagogue up until the present, the church has had to live with and try to understand this tragic fact of history. "He came to his own home, and his own people received him not" (1:11). There were some, says the writer, who believed but out of fear of loss of face and place, they never acknowledged it openly (vv. 42–43). In more than one place, the early church turned to the Jewish Scriptures, and to Isaiah 6:9–10 in particular, to explain to itself how and why the movement initiated by Jesus among his own people became predominantly Gentile by the third generation (Mark 4:12; Matt 13:10–15; Acts 28:26–28; John 12:37–40). As with the preaching of Isaiah, the ministry of Jesus blinded eyes and hardened hearts. Every preacher who has spoken the truth must acknowledge this painful other side to the ministry.

Is this, then, the last word about the public ministry of Jesus? Are the readers to understand that they have the authorization of Jesus to close all missions to Israel? No, not at all. The *very* last paragraph (vv. 44–50) opens with the words,

"And Jesus cried out and said . . . ." The expression, "cried out" is significant. All the signs are over, the debates have ceased, and Jesus stands before the turned backs of unbelief. All exhausted reason, all apparently wasted signs, all spent energies speak with one voice: "You tried; it failed; walk away." But the Evangelist's camera turns one last time upon Jesus, and there he stands in Jerusalem, shouting in a loud voice a final call of faith. The content of that call need not be examined; it consists of a summary of what had been said repeatedly from the beginning. What is important now is the image: Jesus crying out to Israel.

Hopefully, the Johannine church could not and did not lose that final image, but kept it as the model for its own patient, persistent mission. We do not know about the Johannine church, but we do know about ourselves. For the disciples of Jesus the image still lingers, as vivid as ever. There is the word of judgment but it is not the last word. When it seems that there is nothing more to be said, there remains one other word, the word of grace. "And Jesus cried out and said,' . . . I have come as light into the world, that whoever believes in me may not remain in darkness' " (vv. 44, 46).

JESUS, THE REVEALER OF GOD, RETURNS TO GLORY
(JOHN 13:1–20:31)

The Farewell Meal With the Disciples
(John 13:1–30)

Before engaging chapter 13 proper, a few comments introducing the entire unit (chaps. 13–20) might be helpful. The discussion will hang upon three topics: the quantity of this material, the content of it, and its literary form.

Even the casual reader of this Gospel is struck by the fact that the public ministry of Jesus ends at chapter 12 and yet the narrative continues for nine more chapters. Granted, this Evangelist joins the others in giving major attention to the passion story; after all, that was the heart of the Gospel which gave meaning to all else remembered about Jesus. But this account does not begin until chapter 18 and consists of three chapters, whereas five chapters are given to pre-passion speeches and conversations of Jesus. Why?

More than any other Gospel, this one addresses the first major crisis of the church: the departure of Jesus. This writer is more sensitive to, or has seen greater need to address, the darker side of Easter. To be sure, Easter was triumph and vindication, but the announcement of Easter, "He is risen," was prefaced by a less exultant one: "He is not here." That expression captures the pain and the problem. Jesus has been raised and has ascended to glory, but his disciples are still here. Now what? Clearly the problem is not that his followers doubted the resurrection; on the contrary, believing it was the source of difficulty. It was all well and good that Jesus was vindicated and now enjoyed the presence of God, but does his departure mean that the program failed? Are

they to continue? If so, how? Who will lead, and where, to do
what? Are they to look for another? It takes no imagination
to see how vulnerable this group is to false Christs, claimers
to be the new incarnation, prophets passing along messages
which the exalted Lord had given to them in dreams, visions
and states of ecstasy. Before the departing Christ, the disciples had been as children playing on the floor, only to look up
and see the parents putting on coats and hats. The questions
are three (and they have not changed): Where are you going?
Can we go? Then who is going to stay with us?

Chapters 13-17 address those questions. The only other
Gospel writer to deal at length with them is Luke, and he
does so in two ways. One, the risen Christ remains forty days
with his followers, reminding and preparing (Acts 1:1–5).
Two, Luke continues the story of Jesus with a second volume,
detailing how the disciples, after receiving the promised
Spirit (Lk 24:49; Acts 1:4–5), continued the mission of Christ
in the world. The Fourth Evangelist has no second volume,
nor the confirming presence of the risen Christ for forty days.
Rather, compressed into what seems to be one night prior to
his arrest, Jesus is portrayed as preparing them by exempla-
ry act, discourse and prayer for his approaching departure.
These chapters may, therefore, be appropriately entitled,
"Farewell."

As indicated in the paragraphs above, the content of
these chapters falls broadly into two parts: the farewell materials preparing the disciples for the departure of Jesus and
the farewell itself, consisting of the passion story from arrest
to resurrection. As we will have occasion to notice, the passion narrative is remarkably similar to the accounts in the
Synoptics. There are a number of noticeable differences but
the basic story is enough the same to give credence to the
widely held opinion that the passion narrative was the first
unit of material about Jesus to become fixed tradition, resis-
tant to any major modification. The farewell materials prior
to the arrest (chaps. 13-17) will give, in addition to the expected warnings, charges, counsel and encouragement, a
great deal of attention to the granting of the Holy Spirit to
the church to serve as "another Counselor" (14:16) in the
place of Jesus. Sermons on chapters 13-17 would do well to
do the same, not only because of its importance in this Gos-

pel but because of both the interest and the confusion surrounding the topic of the Holy Spirit in the church today.

The third and final statement in introducing chapters 13-20 has to do with the form of the material. Unlike the first twelve chapters, here Jesus speaks directly to the church. Earlier, in the presentation of Jesus' public ministry, the Evangelist, although ever conscious of the readers, had put them in the position of observing and overhearing as Jesus ministered by sign and word among his contemporaries. The burden on the readers of chapters 1-12, therefore, was to find themselves and to hear the message themselves very much as one would in attendance at a play. This method of communication is most effective for those who really watch and listen, but it does tend to "weed out" those who are unwilling or unable to accept the responsibility for hearing the word. Of course, those readers in the Johannine church (and today) who moved close enough to be within understanding distance recognized themselves in the stories and heard in the discourses a very clear word. They discerned, as did we, that even though chapters 1-12 were accounts of the earthly ministry of Jesus, those accounts were being re-told with the church of the readers in mind. In other words, what Jesus said during his ministry and what the risen Lord is saying to his followers become in this Gospel not two messages but one. For two very important reasons, the Lord thus is presented as speaking to the church by means of a re-telling of the ministry of Jesus. One, the church needed and needs the authorization of Jesus Christ himself for its mission, its message, its life and its relation to those who oppose the church. Two, it was and is vitally important for the church to be in continuity with the work and words of Jesus and his apostles. The Johannine church understood itself to be led by the Spirit of God, but such a claim could be and has been made by many groups with conflicting beliefs, practices, and values. By what canons can truth be pulled from the meshes of error? One such canon is continuity with Jesus. As the writer will insist in the materials before us, no spirit that is not in continuity with the work and words of Jesus is the Spirit of truth. By addressing the church by means of the accounts of Jesus' earthly ministry, the Evangelist is both establishing and claiming that continuity, preserved not only by the Spirit which Jesus has given the church, but also by a very

close disciple and associate of Jesus, "the disciple whom Jesus
loved" (13:21–26;   18:15–18;   19:25–27;   20:1–9;   21:4–7;
21:20–24).

But the relation of Christ to the church—that is, to the
reader—will now be noticeably different. Especially in chapters 13–17, the crowds are gone, the opponents are gone, and
Jesus moves inside the church, sits down, and speaks directly. And the preacher, planning the messages to come out of
these chapters, might well spend time on form as well as content, and by the forms of the sermons help the listeners experience the move into the farewell materials. In fact, the
farewell speech is itself an excellent form for proclamation.
Both Testaments know it quite well: recall the farewell addresses of Moses, Joshua, Stephen, Paul (to the elders from
Ephesus), and now Jesus.

"Now before the feast of the Passover" (13:1), begins the
Evangelist. The reader is thereby informed that the last meal
was not the Passover meal as in the Synoptics (Mark 14:12,
par.), stopping at the outset any anticipation of the eucharist,
and preparing for the description of Jesus' dying as the Passover lamb (19:31–37). In other words, Jesus does not *eat* the

Passover, he *is* the Passover. This Gospel's Passover meal
with the attendant eucharistic interpretation was presented
in chapter 6. Whether the writer intends 13:1 as a correction
of the Synoptics, or is using a different source, or is sacrific-
ing chronology to theology is much debated in the commentaries. Regardless of one's position on that issue, totally
unaffected is the writer's own presentation of the
significance of that evening. The supper itself functions as
the scene for what is said and done by Jesus. He interrupts
the meal to wash the disciples' feet (vv. 2–5), an event not
understood (v. 7) even though it is followed by two interpretations (vv. 6–11, 12–20), and to point out the betrayer with
the offer of the dipped morsel (vv. 21–27), which also was not
understood (vv. 28–30).

The Evangelist wants the reader to understand what the
twelve did not understand. First, Jesus knows fully what he is
doing and, as usual, is completely in charge. Notice: "Jesus,
knowing that the Father had given all things into his hands"
(v. 3); "for he knew who was to betray him" (v. 11); and , "I

know whom I have chosen" (v. 18). That Jesus is fully in charge is dramatized by the fact that Jesus not only knows Judas will betray him, but Jesus actually commands him: "What you are going to do, do quickly" (v. 27). Whatever inroads into the reader's views of free will these lines may make, they were undoubtedly intended to give confidence and engender faith (v. 19) in disciples who otherwise could view the events of this night (betrayal and arrest) as defeat. These lines not only encouraged the first readers who could parallel in their own experience nights of betrayal and arrest, but also gave them a way to witness in the face of otherwise silencing questions: Did not your leader's close associates betray him? Was not your leader executed as a criminal?

But even those of us who witness without threat of public embarrassment or violence are not unmoved by the writer's description of Jesus that night. Jesus was fully aware of his origin in glory, says the Evangelist; he was also aware that he was now returning to that eternal glory in God's presence; and he was further aware that while on earth, all authority from God was his. In other words, the writer turns up the lights to their brightest, all focused on Jesus in the sweeping affirmation: from God, to God, possessing all knowledge and power. In that dazzling moment what will he say? Will he command his followers to bow down in worship before him? What will he do? Will he ascend in a cloud out of their sight? He rose from the table, replaced his robe with a towel, poured water in a basin, washed the disciples' feet and dried them with the towel around his waist. What this means for the church's understanding of itself has not really soaked in yet.

Apparently two interpretations are offered. The first (vv. 6–11) insists that the church is in the posture of recipient, having its nature and character in the self-giving act of Jesus. The church is the church by his grace. It is this understanding which Simon Peter (and many since) resisted. As a representative of the church which does not get the point, Simon Peter does not want his feet washed by his Teacher and Lord. The second interpretation (vv. 12–20) understands that act of Jesus as a model of humility and service which the church is to emulate. In theory if not in practice this has been the interpretation most commonly accepted, perhaps because giving service is easier than receiving it. It is not as though the two interpretations are necessarily independent of each other. On the contrary, in a healthy state the church would implement the second because it accepted the first.

The preacher might be interested in pursuing other interpretations by which the church appropriated the scene. For example, in areas of strong sacramentalism, the supper and the washing are understood as eucharist and baptism. In other quarters, and especially during persecutions, the supper and the washing have been understood as the Johannine parallel to the call to martyrdom in Mark: "Are you able to drink the cup that I drink, or to be baptized with the baptism with which I am baptized?" (10:38). Except for a few denominations, the church has not taken literally Christ's command to follow his example, and therefore footwashing has not been accorded sacramental status. But there is no interpretation that can obscure in 13:1-30 the three strong messages against the spiritual arrogance and triumphalism which, for some strange reason, have always plagued the church and contradicted the Gospel: the Lord's washing his followers' feet, the prideful resistance of disciples who do not understand, and the treachery within the inner circle ("He who ate my bread has lifted his heel against me," v. 18; Ps 41:9).

It was this last matter, the treason of Judas, which, after the death of Jesus by crucifixion, put the heaviest burden upon those who interpreted the story for the church. Next to Jesus, the person of Judas is the strongest magnet drawing the attention of both writer and reader in all three paragraphs of this section.

Rather than speculating on the reasons for his act (love of money, political disappointment, attempting to provoke Jesus into a move against the establishment, schizophrenia, demon possession, etc.) the church would better spend its time responding as Mark says the twelve did: "They began to be sorrowful, and to say to him one after another, 'Is it I?' " (14:19).

Three comments of the Evangelist in vv. 21-30 grab the reader's attention and, while perhaps not deserving lengthy treatment by the preacher, certainly could add appropriate detail and color to sermons from this passage. The first is the description of Jesus as "troubled in spirit" (v. 21). This could well be a statement of the same nature as 11:33; that is, the emotional state of Jesus is disturbed by the events immediately before him, in this case, the departure of a close associate to make a pact with the enemy. While it is true Jesus had several times earlier referred to his betrayal, such moments from a distance never have the same ugly countenance as when viewed across the supper table. But an alternate reading of "troubled in spirit" is to understand it as a description of the prophetic state. This view is supported by the unusual verb which follows: "He was troubled in spirit and *testified*." That word distinguishes the statement of Jesus which follows from the usual "Jesus said."

The second comment in this paragraph so unusual as to draw our attention is the reference to "one of his disciples, whom Jesus loved" (v. 23). This unnamed disciple appears in six scenes in chapters 13–21, and except for the one at the cross with Jesus' mother (19:25–27), all will be in the company of Simon Peter (13:21–26; 18:15–18; 20:1–9; 21:4–7; 21:20–24). The commentaries will discuss all of history's guesses as to who this disciple is. Just now it probably is enough to notice this person was especially close to Jesus; this person provides the Johannine church with continuity with Jesus and gives it apostolic authority; this person always precedes Simon Peter in knowledge, in faith and in relation to Jesus. If it is historically appropriate to speak of Johannine and Petrine circles of Christinanity, then this writer is confident as to who was and is closest to the heart and truth of the Jesus tradition. Peter is not rejected by any means; he and his are simply put in what this Evangelist considers "their place."

The third and final comment does not so much inform as it teases: "and it was night" (v. 30). One suspects here, as at 3:2, not so much a reference to the clock as to the nature of the act. However, it is interesting that in the earliest known tradition related to the eucharist, the designation of Judas' act as occurring at night is preserved: "the Lord Jesus on the night when he was betrayed took bread" (1 Cor 11:23).

The Farewell Discourses
(John 13:31–17:26)

We begin here a unit of material that does not end until 17:26. The preacher is faced with two difficulties in determining the best way to chart the sub-divisions within this lengthy section. One problem lies in the fact that there are few points within the material where natural breaks are marked by the usual transition clues: change of time, change of location, or shift in activity. We have here no change of time or place and no activity. Even efforts by commentaries to re-arrange this chapter do not grant relief here. The second difficulty lies within the material itself. There are frequent and lengthy repetitions which have been accounted for in a variety of ways. Perhaps repetition was intended for emphasis, or is the result of joining sources that preserved discourses of Jesus different enough to keep even at the price of monotony, or is due to the Gospel having passed through several editions in the course of its formation. Whatever the reason for it, the material in this section is too important to be handled so as to close ears and turn listeners away with such comments as "But that was the same as last Sunday's sermon" or "Pastor, you have already made that point; why not move on?" It would be advisable, therefore, even when the intent is to move chapter by chapter through the Gospel, to preach somewhat thematically, letting messages draw upon the clusters of texts which respond to the primary question of this entire section: What does the departing Christ have to say to his church?

The Farewell Announcement (13:31–38)

Predictions of the passion of Jesus have been so dramatically and almost shockingly presented in the Gospel of Mark (and in Matt and Luke, with modification) that the quiet prediction of John 13:31–38 can be easily overlooked. While the Evangelist joins the Synoptics in saying that the announcement of Jesus met with confusion and resistance among the disciples (Mark 8:27–33; 9:30–37; 10:32–45), there are few other similarities. In Mark the predictions are in private; here the disciples are told what had already been said to the Jews (v. 33). In Mark, arrest, suffering, death and resurrection are spelled out; here Jesus is going away in a little while (vv. 33, 36). In Mark, the predictions are followed by calls to crossbearing, servanthood and childlikeness; here Jesus commands that they love one another (vv. 34–35). If Mark is calling the church to the way of the cross, what is this Evangelist saying by the manner and content of Jesus' announcement that now is the hour of departure?

It is quite evident that the key to the passage before us is relationship. The announcement of his approaching death presupposes that the relationship of the group to Jesus is primary, and Jesus seeks to translate that relationship of the disciples to him to a fellowship that exists *among them*, characterized by love. Notice the language: "Little children"; "yet a little while I am with you"; "you will seek me"; "where I am going you cannot follow me now; but you shall follow afterward"; "Lord, why cannot I follow you now?" This is family talk, painful conversation in a circle of friends about to lose the one who is their reason for being together. It almost seems like an effort to explain death to the children in the family. We should not, however, regard the treatment of death as "going away" as euphemistic avoidance of the ugly truth. Throughout the Gospel, the death of Jesus has been called "going away," "going to my Father" and "being glorified," and all for the simple reason that this *is* what is happening to Jesus. For this Evangelist, the death itself is not so intrinsically meaningful; death rather is the means by which Jesus returns to his former glory. His being lifted up is, of course, on the cross, but he is being lifted up in a far more significant sense. To be sure, the writer will provide an interpretation of Jesus' death on the cross, but theories of atonement or of the moral influence of his dying are much more evident in other New Testament writers than here. It is best that such views not be imported to burden the text.

What is worthy of reflection is the fact that Jesus says here to his followers what he had said earlier to the Jews and yet it is evident that the words, although exactly the same, have an entirely different meaning. Why? Because relationship determines meaning. Words whispered in a family are not the same when shouted on the street. Words of a friend are not the same when quoted by an enemy. Those who love us can say what those who do not love us never can. A preacher who is also a good pastor and a preacher who is aloof say different things with the same words. Let the preacher, then, keep in mind that 13:31–38 is inside talk, church talk, and is not very meaningful over the loud speaker in a parking lot. The care of words as well as the care of souls is a responsibility of the ministry.

The concern of Jesus in this text is that their relationship to him inform and determine their relationship to each other. Jesus is leaving and nothing will be gained by longing after him, or by thinking this is the end of everything, or that life is now stale, flat and tasteless, without meaning. As he had loved them, they are to love each other, and in this way the witness will continue to be made to the world. The "one another" of the words of Jesus here quite clearly refers to the disciples, the community of faith. There are times and there are texts that call for love in a larger circle, but not here. Here love is the cement to hold together the community of faith. Love for those within and love for those without are not mutually exclusive. The error lies in allowing the one to excuse us from the other. But apparently an immediate need in the Johannine community (and to this we will return in chap. 17) was internal love and harmony. Whether the problem in the church lay in the area of personality conflicts or doctrinal disputes or tensions created by outside pressures is not clear from the Gospel itself, but whatever the cause, its elimination was considered essential to the continued life of the community as disciples of Jesus.

Two words characterizing the love they are to have for each other are difficult and require much thought. The words are "new commandment." In what sense "new"? Certainly not new in the sense that love for one another was heretofore absent from their lives or their traditions in Judaism. Perhaps it was new in the sense that Jesus had not until the time of his departure spoken this way to them. Perhaps it was new in that the era before them, a time of continuing Jesus' work in his absence, was new and called for a new understanding of themselves. Or it may have been new in that the love they had for each other was to be patterned after his love for

them. And why "commandment"? Can love be commanded?
The word does sound out of place, especially to those of us
who have not only deleted "command" and "obey" from our
vocabularies but who also use "love" in terms of emotion. To
command emotions would most likely be counterproductive.
But what if love is not an emotion? What if love is the way
God acts toward the world and the way Jesus acts toward his
disciples? In that case we are talking about telling the truth,
being faithful in sharing the word of God, continuing to act
for those who may not be responsive, and, if need be, giving
one's life. If this is love, then the word of Jesus here moves us
out of naming our feelings and tinkering with our psyches
and into speaking and doing for one another.

The Farewell Promises (14:1—15:11)

It was suggested above that the preacher handle the
material in 13:31—17:26 thematically as a way to achieve
thoroughness without excessive repetition. Such has been
the attempt here and in the two following subsections. We
want always to acknowledge the limitations of such divisions even when we use them. For example, gathering
14:1—15:11 under the heading "Farewell Promises" does
not mean that all here are promises nor that all the promises are here. Nor is it to be implied that 14:1—15:11 can best
be treated in one message. That could be done; many sermons, long or short, lack not so much truth as size. However, reasons for detecting and respecting smaller units
within this passage are not only practical but also textual.
Some of the statements of Jesus here are self-contained
truths having their integrity without dependence upon present context. In fact, some of them may have had a pre-Gos-
pel existence in entirely different contexts, as, for example,
14:1–3 or 14:6 or 14:16–17. For our purposes here, what
seem to be natural breaks in the text will be honored:
14:1–14; 14:15–24; 14:25–31; 15:1–11.

The primary concern of the farewell discourses is not
what events are to befall Christ but what will happen to his
disciples. It is not surprising, then, that the first thrust of this
material is to soften with assurance the blow of the announcement of his departure. In vv. 1–14, the promises are
three. First, there is the promise of a place, a permanent

abiding place with the Son in God's house. There is no doubt
that the image here is of the future, a fact which in no way
erases the present or realized eschatology of other passages.
The word translated "rooms" (RSV), "dwelling places"
(NEB) or "mansions" (KJV) is the noun form of the word "to
abide." We have already seen, and will be reminded in
14:1–11, how significant the word is for this Evangelist. It
represents a relationship characterized by trusting and even
knowing, comparable to the relation of Christ to God. Such
trusting and knowing are possibilities for the disciples and
will, according to this text, be fulfilled rather than severed at
death. If the fundamental human longing is to know God, the

epitome of human fulfillment would be to be with God. The
picture of being with God in a prepared place is not peculiar
to this passage. Some Jewish writers list heaven and hell as
two of the seven things God prepared before creating the
world. Abraham is described in the Epistle to the Hebrews as
seeking not just a land but a homeland, "the city which has
foundations, whose builder and maker is God" (11:10).

The second promise is of the way to God. The preacher
will want to avoid being seduced by what appears to be a
ready made sermon outline: the way, the truth, the life (v. 6).
It is clear from the context that the conversation among
Jesus, Thomas, and Philip has to do with God, being with
God, and the way to that place with God. In vv. 5–6 the subject is the way and whatever is made of Jesus as truth and
life must serve the central issue of the way to God. And for
this Evangelist, here and throughout the Gospel, the way to
God whom no one has ever seen is through the revelation of
God in the Son. The Johannine community is clear on this.
What is not clear is whether the expression "no one comes to
the Father, but by me" (v. 6) is a polemic, and if so, against
whom. One can rather safely assume the writer's awareness
of both the synagogue and the Baptist sect in such a statement, but in view of the statements about the Holy Spirit
(14:15—16:15), the remark about Jesus as the only way to
God could be addressed to pneumatics or charismatics who
discounted the historical Jesus in favor of new revelations in
the Spirit. If an interpreter extends the meaning of "no one
comes to the Father, but by me" as a polemic against other
religions (Moslem, Hindu, etc.), then responsibility must be

taken for that application rather than giving the impression
that this was what the Evangelist had in mind.

The third promise in 14:1–14 is that of an adequacy, a
power, for the meanwhile; that is, for the life of the believing
community in the world, prior to abiding forever in God's
house. The promise is to those who believe in the Son and
pray in his name (vv. 13–14). The commentaries will docu-
ment from the Old Testament and other literature the common belief in the power resident in one's name and the
responsibilities involved in using someone's name. Let it be
noted here that the use of Jesus' name as authorization for
prayers to God is to be taken no less seriously, and clearly
implies that those who do so know Christ and abide in Christ
and make their requests from that context. In fact, the
prayers will be native to that relationship rather than selfish
intrusions from another value system. And what is assumed
here about the context of the community's prayers? They are
not pleas for the power to cope privately, to survive privately, to be rewarded privately. The use of plural "you" (vv.
13–14) implies the community of faith, and the aim of the
church's prayers is the continuation of Jesus' work. The
promise is that the church will not have to survive on the
memory of what Jesus did while he was there, but will be
able to maintain and even enlarge upon that work. What the
church is enabled to do is "the works that I do" (v. 12). These
works are not spelled out, but it would not be wise for the
preacher to fill in the silence with favorite descriptions of
Jesus' ministry from sources other than the Fourth Gospel.
Let the preacher stay inside this Gospel and have the imagination disciplined by pressing the question, What does Jesus
do, *according to the Gospel of John?* Doubtless the sermon
which results will focus upon the way in which God is revealed and made present among us in word and act. Such a
sermon will make clear what the text makes clear: his promise to the church is his commission to the church.

The statement "and greater works than these will he do,
because I go to the Father" (v. 12) introduces the discussion
of the Holy Spirit, which begins in the next section,
14:15–24. Here again the interpreter is impressed not only by
the wealth of the passage but also by its resistance to being
minted into small coins. However, even at the risk of reduc-

tionism, some way of taking hold of this text by both preacher and listener has to be found. It might be helpful to distinguish between the wealth of the text's offering and the locked doors behind which it is kept. The opening (v. 15) and closing (v. 24) sentences guard the contents of the passage, announcing clearly that there is nothing here for passersby, those of "the world" who lack the faith and the insight to appropriate what is available (v. 17). The keys for unlocking the door to the treasure are love and obedience. That relationship to God characterized as love that keeps commandments, of which we have spoken earlier, is the absolute precondition for receiving Christ's gift to his followers.

What is offered to those who love obediently may be called a Johannine form of Pentecost and the Parousia (the coming of Christ). In the sense that Pentecost has come to refer to the giving of the Holy Spirit to the disciples, vv. 16–17 describe Pentecost, even though lacking the imagery and remarkable signs of Acts 2:1–13. In spite of the differences in description, the two accounts agree that Easter is completed at Pentecost; without the giving of the Spirit, Easter is not just resurrection but final departure.

But the promise, though brief, is clear: upon his departure Jesus will ask God to replace him with the Spirit to be in and with the church. Unlike Jesus, the Spirit will not go away, but like Jesus, the Spirit will provide truth (about God and life eternal) and counsel or help. Peculiar to this Gospel is the designation of the Spirit of God as Paraclete, that is, Counselor, Helper or Comforter. In that the Spirit is "another Counselor" the Spirit is to be to the church what Jesus had been to his disciples.

However, vv. 18–24 make it clear that one should not attempt to distinguish too sharply between the coming of the Spirit and the coming of Christ (parousia). "I will not leave you desolate (literally, orphans): I will come to you " (v. 18). The presence of the Spirit with the church and the presence of Christ are not differentiated. In fact, v. 23 includes within that promise the presence also of God. When Jesus says that he and God "will come to him and make our *home* with him," he uses the word translated in v. 2 as "rooms." With care the preacher can bless rather than confuse the congregation with this two-fold eschatology: we will get to dwell with

God (v. 2); in the meantime, God comes to dwell with us (v. 23). And whether or not this passage yields two sermons, Pentecost and parousia, or only one is a decision to be made in each case by those whose responsibility it is to feed the flock of God. Whatever the decision, that the two doctrines are experientially one for the Johannine community is a truth which should not be withheld from the church today simply out of fear that the truth and benefits of a doctrine of the future coming of Christ be lost.

Attention to 14:25–31 should focus primarily upon the statement about the Holy Spirit (v. 26), the second in a series of five, the first having been given in 14:16–17. This is not to say the remainder of the paragraph is unimportant but that it continues and repeats the mood of comfort in the hour of departure. Here the words of assurance consist of the granting of God's peace and a re-assertion that the events of arrest and death soon to transpire are in no sense a triumph of the world. On the contrary, they are better understood as the operation of God's will in all circumstances and of the Son's full obedience of love. The peace that is given is not as the world gives; that is, it is not a truce with one's environment whereby hassles are avoided and comfortable nests are undisturbed. It is not "getting away on weekends" to a mountain lake or a strip of private beach, as attractive as that may be. The peace of God is the confidence that God is God and neither our gains nor our losses are ultimate. It is the trust that God loves the world, is *for* all creatures, and is present with us in every endeavor to make real that love in concrete ways. Hassles as we go through life neither prove nor disprove God's presence and therefore neither create nor void the peace of God.

The closing line of this paragraph, "Rise, let us go thence," has generated no small discussion among scholars. Some take it to mean that at this point Jesus and his disciples leave the supper table and move toward the garden where he was betrayed. Others regard this statement as further evidence in favor of re-arranging the discourses in this section so that "Rise, let us go hence" concludes the farewell conversations and immediately precedes 18:1: "When Jesus had spoken these words, he went forth with his disciples across the Kidron valley...." Neither handling of the line

materially alters the message of the paragraph. The preacher
could well treat 14:25–31 as the Evangelist's rather elaborate
parallel to the brief farewell scenes in Matthew ("and lo, I
am with you always," 28:20) and Luke ("While he blessed
them, he parted from them," 24:51).

We return now to v. 26 and the teaching about the Paraclete, the Holy Spirit. It is especially important for ministers
to teach and to preach on the subject since some churches
are intimidated by it and others are indulging in it. Recent
discussions of the Holy Spirit among Christians have tended
to begin and end with 1 Cor 12 and Paul's treatment of char-
ismatic gifts in Corinth, letting that passage draw like a magnet texts on the Holy Spirit from the remainder of the New
Testament. The error of this procedure is that it does not allow other principal writers on the subject (Luke and John
primarily) to present their own distinct perspectives. A minister in a context such as this may choose to treat the Paraclete sayings in this Gospel in a series of messages that will
not only instruct but provide an alternative to what in some
quarters has become an unsettling fixation upon the charismatics in Corinth.

In v. 26 the Evangelist says four things about the Spirit
which obviously were considered important for the readers
to understand and which remain instructive for us. One, the
Holy Spirit is given, not "gotten." While we cannot with certainty reconstruct the conditions calling for the repeated reminder that *God* sends the Spirit, we can rather safely
imagine, given the whole New Testament's struggle with
claims of Spirit possession, demonstrations of Spirit possession, and even one case of an attempt to purchase the Spirit
(Acts 8:18–20). In this regard, little has changed: audiences
are manipulated to "get the Spirit"; announcements request
"those who want the Holy Spirit remain after the benediction" and advertisements promise that a cassette tape or-
dered by mail gives "step-by-step instructions on how to get
the Holy Spirit." That God gives the Spirit is a natural corol-
lary to salvation by grace; that there is a way we can get it is
blasphemous arrogance. The second and third statements
about the Paraclete are similar: the Spirit is in Jesus' name
and will "bring to your remembrance all that I have said to
you." As stated earlier, the Holy Spirit is not a direct and

immediate experience of God which qualifies one to disregard or reject the historical Jesus, the apostolic tradition, or the church. To be sure, one does not uncritically embrace every tradition bearing the name Christian nor give unqualified allegiance to the institutional church in order to have the Spirit, but neither does one dismiss out of hand "all that garbage" in favor of a nice, warm "just me and God" experience of the Spirit. Being a Christian is to a certain extent an exercise of memory, and a function of the Spirit is to enroll believers in the story of God's word in the world.

Not far afield was an early Christian definition for being lost; it was "to have amnesia." And the fourth statement is, the Holy Spirit "will teach you all things." Why more teaching? Because new conditions and circumstances call for hearing anew and appropriating anew the word of Christ. The Gospel is not only old but new, rooted in Israel and yet indigenous to every place and time. The Holy Spirit in the church keeps the tradition a living word. The Holy Spirit is not simply a feeling; the words here speak of instruction and content. We are not nourished by chewing, but by chewing food.

The last unit in this section is 15:1–11. If the preacher finds 15:1–6 a more congenial unit, a number of commentaries will agree, considering v. 7 the point at which the vine and branches analogy shifts into the more familiar Johannine categories of love and obedience. Others will support a larger unit of vv. 1–17 on the basis of the appearance of the radical shift in content at v. 18. However, the introduction of the word "friends" to replace "servants" (vv. 12–17) as a description of the disciples is subject matter enough to separate vv. 1–11 from the instruction that begins at v. 12.

The controlling image in vv. 1–11 is the vineyard, and especially the vine. Like the shepherd image in chap. 10, the vineyard evokes associations and meanings familiar to those readers if not to some of us. The commentaries will provide a wealth of background material from Jewish and Christian sources that form the reservoir out of which this text is drawn. Again, like the shepherd image, the vine and branches is neither an allegory nor a parable, but more correctly in Johannine terms, a figure (in contrast to plain or direct speech). The controlling verb in this passage is "abide," already in this Gospel a rich and full word to describe a relationship of trust, love, knowledge and that oneness characteristic of God and Christ. Here, however, the word reaches its peak in frequency of use and in intensity of meaning. After all, the life-giving, fruit-bearing relation of a vine and its branches hardly needs explanation, much less argument. Sermons that explain and illustrate this point are not only dull but insult the intelligence. What can be pointed out as instructive and helpful is that the relation between Christ and his followers here in this analogy is not a future one. It is a here and now relationship, not some mystic union in a great elsewhere. And the single point of the discussion is fruitbearing. What fruit is meant here is not spelled out, but one should not, therefore, rush to a concordance to find the references to "fruit." Earlier the Evangelist referred to fruit-bearing in connection with the Christian message among the nations (12:20–27). That could hardly be an inappropriate interpretation here; certainly one to be preferred over trips inward and subjective explorations often launched by this text.

It probably would be helpful to try experiencing this text before using it to exhort ourselves and others. Be a branch and feel the knife of the vinedresser. Both dead branches and live branches are severely cut, in the one case in order to be tossed away, in the other for the purpose of increased fruitfulness. Experientially, what is the difference? Interestingly, the Greek words translated "to take away" and "to prune" have the same stem. "Every branch of mine that bears no fruit, *airei* (he takes away), and every branch that does bear fruit, *athairei* (he prunes) that it may bear more fruit" (v. 2). The play on words stirs the readers to realize how similar and yet how different are the two experiences of the vinedresser's cutting. Pruning can be so painful (removal of the debilitating baggage of things, relationships, activities, meaningless pursuits). Who among us has not interpreted the experience as being cut away from God, hurt, angry, and confused? Quite likely the Johannine church needed to be reminded that their present pains could be understood as pruning for more fruitfulness. Churches that move through hardship to increased devotion to the mission have, indeed, been pruned. Those that pull back in fear and resentment with attention only to their own comfort and safety have, indeed, been taken away.

The Farewell Instructions and Warnings
(15:12–16:33)

The opening paragraph of this section forms what is sometimes called an inclusion—that is, a distinct literary unit which ends as it begins. In this case, v. 12 and v. 17 are the same: the disciples are commanded to love one another. Between those two verses is a new theme in the discourses of Jesus. Three times Jesus refers to his disciples as friends. It is a beautiful expression, recalling the reference to Abraham as the friend of God, but it can also be a dangerously misleading statement. Jesus' calling the disciples "my friends" is not a reference to their character as though somehow they had moved to a new level of sanctification. Neither is it a designation of office or station; there is no upward mobility in the Kingdom whereby a disciple can eventually graduate from servant and become one of the spiritual elite, the friends of Jesus. Disciples never cease to be servants any more than Jesus ever quit serving; otherwise, the footwashing and instruction at the Last Supper were meaningless. The text makes it clear that the disciples are friends because, unlike servants, friends know what the family is doing (v. 15). Jesus has shared with them knowledge of God and the word of God. The revelation of who God is creates a community around the One who made God known and that community, formed by the Word, is here called "the friends of Jesus." Elitism must be avoided even though that is an ever-present danger wherever there exists that strong sense of community as is evident in this Gospel.

Herein lies the danger mentioned earlier. All the raw materials for the alienating arrogance which has never ceased to plague the church are to be found here: a knowledge of the truth; an unbroken tradition that goes back to Jesus; persecution from the world which confirms the uniqueness of the community; and a strong commitment to mutual love within the group. Where these qualities prevail there may be found a very strong church. But strangely enough, these same qualities may be claimed by groups which by attitude and behavior actually hinder the witness and mission of the Christ in whose name they meet. For example, the claim that "our church is like a family" may be an

offer of love and acceptance, but in some cases it has proved
to be a way of saying, "We reserve the right to refuse service
to anyone." Truth and error often dress alike.

In sharp contrast to 15:1–17 with its "inside" words of
love, abiding, and friendship, 15:18–16:4a describes what is
going on "outside." In this section the key words are hate,
persecute, sin, expel and kill. These comments about the
world out there appear at a most appropriate place in the
discourse, for without them the preceding paragraphs could
lure the church into becoming a Christian ghetto. Without
them the church could also draw its chairs into a circle and
become so preoccupied with intramurals that it forgets there
is another force to be reckoned with: the world.

Here let us properly warn ourselves. Unless we stay on
guard, texts like this which portray the world as the hostile
force over against the church may be used by the preacher to
justify a general sense of resentment toward all those people
out there who do not attend our churches nor come to hear
our sermons. Texts that indict the world may be used to bless
that vague sense of envy harbored by some ministers who
stand at the window of a forgotten parish and watch a sleek
and fat world cruise past, on its way not to perdition but to a
party. Not a few ministers find shouting these texts to anyone who will listen the only relief from chronic bitterness.
Looking more carefully at the text before us is one way to
protect ourselves from such disasters.

The section 15:18–16:4a does not caress a martyr complex nor license the church to rail against the world. The
passage is descriptive not imperative; it states what is happening and what will happen to the followers of Jesus.
There are no instructions on how to get people to hate
Christians but rather the clear-eyed statement that the disciples are not exempt from the treatment accorded their
Lord. The Johannine community needed to understand
their own persecution and expulsion from the synagogue in
this way, lest they fall away or stumble in their discipleship
(16:1). It was not then, nor is it now, difficult to begin interpreting hardship as being abandoned by God, and if God
abandons us, then we must be wrong. Such a theological
assessment is reinforced when the persecutors are invoking
the name of God and quoting Scripture as divine authoriza-

tion for their actions (16:2). Within the memory of adult Americans, murders have been wrapped in Scripture, hymns and prayer, with church buildings serving as meeting places for the perpetrators.

Let the preacher, then, think carefully before pronouncing "world" in the sermon. When this Evangelist says it, he is not looking down a dark street lined with casinos and houses of ill repute. There are texts aplenty for the pulpit in that parish, but not in the Gospel of John. Here one is looking down a well-lighted street lined with respected institutions. What, then, is the problem? For this Evangelist the world created and loved of God has grown blind and deaf to its Creator and now protects its own values and agenda from the word God sends to it. That Word, Jesus Christ, reminds the world that its origin, its end, its life is in the Creator. All other values and goods are derived from that. But the world has already had its program printed and since an invocation and benediction by resident clergy are included, any word that calls for change is not only unsettling and intruding but must also be rejected as ungodly.

And so the world's sin (15:22–24) is unbelief, but it is not a quiet, cold, indifferent unbelief. Apparently because it was created through the Word, the world has sufficient recollection of its source to recognize that the Word which Jesus both is and speaks comes from God. Otherwise the Word would strike the unbelieving world as a light bulb strikes a stone wall. But such is not the case. The world, wounded by the Word and pierced by the light, thrashes about, hurting itself and making casualties of those who witness to the truth. The text here does not shrink from acknowledging that the cause of agitation is the Word. Without the word, darkness, slumber and amnesia would appropriately describe a kind of false peace. "If I had not come and spoken to them, they would not have sin; but now they have no excuse for their sin. . . . If I had not done among them the works which no one else did, they would not have sin; but now they have seen and hated both me and my Father" (15:22, 24).

That the Word is a disturbing presence is not a phenomenon confined to this Gospel. The Word in Nazareth aroused prejudices and precipitated an attempt to throw Jesus over a cliff (Luke 4:16–30). The Word in Philippi healed a slave girl but at the same time cut off the income her owners had received from her fortunetelling. Those who spoke that healing Word were subjected to mob brutality, Roman cruelty and the dungeon (Acts 16:16–24). The Word in Ephesus liberated many from magic, superstition and idolatry but the loss to those who sold potions, charms, amulets, and books on how to be healthy, wealthy, and wise was considerable. The price for such liberation was mob action against those who witnessed to the Word (Acts 19:17–41). And today's newspaper joins the New Testament in continuing the story. The missionary who is far from being a revolutionary or even a social activist speaks of the love and grace of God toward every person. The listeners gain a new understanding of themselves and the new self-respect threatens regressive economic and political structures. As a seed carries its own future in its bosom, so does the Word carry its own future and the future of those who hear. Those who witness to the Word need to understand this in order to be prepared for both the peace and the persecution which follow the preaching of the Gospel.

But Jesus promises that these do not witness alone. In the third of the five Holy Spirit sayings Jesus reminds his disciples of the supportive and confirming presence of the Spirit (15:16). That witnessing will draw hostile opposition is a fact the disciples must accept; after all, the servant is not greater than the master (15:20). But the disciples can draw strength in the confidence that the truth gives, that Jesus gives, that God gives, that the Spirit gives. Such surrounding assurance in the midst of extreme circumstances makes the unbearable bearable. Nothing more could be promised. "But I have said these things to you, that when their hour comes you may remember that I told you of them" (16:4a). As was said earlier, being a Christian is at times very much a matter of remembering.

Because 16:4b–33 so closely parallels 13:31–14:31, we need here only to comment on the few statements that are new material. The major commentaries will acquaint those interested with the theories which seek to account for the repetition here of the earlier portion of the discourse. One is struck by the fact that 16:4b–33 seems totally unaware of 13:31–14:31. For example, Jesus says in 16:5 that no one has asked him where he is going and yet that very question was asked in the earlier section, and more than once. Surely we are dealing here with different compositions now joined in the Gospel as it comes to us. As was the case with 13:31–14:31, this section is extremely difficult to divide into smaller units. The usual literary transitions are lacking, but for purposes of handling the material for preaching, a division could be made between vv. 4b-15 and 16-33. To avoid repetition of earlier comments our purposes will be served here by concentrating primarily on the fourth and fifth Holy Spirit sayings found in this section.

The fourth Holy Spirit saying (16:7–11) is the most difficult of the five because it speaks of the Spirit in relation to the world not to the church. The earlier statement that the world does not know and cannot receive the Paraclete (14:17), since the promise of another Counselor is only to the church, makes it imperative to understand the relation of the Spirit to the world not as direct but mediated through the church. The RSV says the work of the Spirit is to "convince the world," giving the clear impression that toward the world the Holy Spirit is a persuading force, an evangelizing power that enables the church to bring the unbelieving world under conviction for the error of its ways. Such a translation has the force of a promise that the blind and hostile world will come to faith; it will be "convinced." That is good to hear, but vv. 8-11 elaborate on what the Spirit does to the world in such a way as to make it clear that judgment for wrong rather than persuasion to the right is the writer's point. The word translated "convince" can also be translated "convict" in the sense of exposing or bringing to light as in a trial. The language is obviously that of a courtroom, especially if "righteousness" of vv. 8, 9 is translated "justice." Righteousness has too strong a moral flavor to fit the context.

Let the preacher, then, bring the listeners into the jury box of the courtroom. The case is clear: the world vs. Jesus of Nazareth. The facts are known: the world determined that Jesus was not from God. On the contrary, it seemed expedient for the peace and stability of the nation that Jesus with his disturbing claims should be eliminated. And so it was that Jesus was put to death with the full consent and encouragement of the religious establishment. In fact, that there was no divine intervention was persuasive argument that justice was served. The case for the world is closed. A function of the Holy Spirit, however, is the enlightenment that offers another reading of the evidence. The world acted toward Jesus in unbelief because he *was* the revealing Word of God. The world acted not justly but unjustly in putting him to death, but in doing so a higher justice was served. By his death Jesus returned to God and sent his followers the Holy Spirit. And the world was not vindicated in its action against Jesus by the clear absence of any divine intervention. On the contrary, not only was God's will served by that crucifixion, but the death of Jesus was a victory over the world. The judges were judged.

Where is this courtroom in which this trial is held and these conclusions reached? Not "out there" somewhere, but in the minds of the disciples. There and nowhere else the issues had to be settled. Absolutely nothing was more crucial to the survival and growth of the church than an understanding of the death of Jesus as something other than the Roman execution of a potential troublemaker in the interests of peace and as insurance against grassroots rebellion. But how was the community of faith able to read the evidence so as to come up with an interpretation other than political expediency? The Fourth Evangelist says that this different understanding of the death of Jesus was the work of the Holy Spirit. As Jesus is the interpreter of God, the Holy Spirit is the interpreter of Jesus, and to the Spirit's interpretation the church is to witness. Such witnessing demands not only faith but courage because the world which does not know the Spirit has its own interpretation. The church must not allow itself to be intimidated into silence because not everyone agrees with its sermon. In the heydey of Christendom when Christianity was the official religion, the church was the only team on the field and could score at will. Such was not the case when this Gospel was written, nor is it today.

The fifth and final Holy Spirit saying (16:13–15) must be handled with care lest the expression "Will guide you into all truth" and "will declare to you the things that are to come" serve as texts to bless every new fad and notion. That the Spirit continues to guide and enlighten the church is a truth of the faith not to be abandoned out of fear of the new and different. Were the church to become so protective and defensive as to force today to serve yesterday, then the present would cease to be God's time and preachers would turn curators. In fact, the Fourth Gospel itself as a radically new interpretation of the meaning of Jesus Christ could be justified only if the Spirit continues in the church the work of interpretation. Communities of faith must be indigenous to their own times and places, pressing always the question, What does Jesus Christ mean today? Quite likely the expression "will declare to you the things that are to come," while certainly a reference to the future from the position of Jesus as speaker, was for the reader a reference to their own situation. There is nothing here to warrant claims about the Spirit as a source of information concerning the eschaton. On the contrary, the word of Jesus to the Johannine church is that the Holy Spirit among them is, even at the time they are reading this Gospel, guiding and enabling them to speak and live the truth in their own situations. But let the church read vv. 13–15 carefully lest Spirit claims lead to theological and ethical license. What has been said often before is again repeated here, for the excesses of a spurious individualism were and are well known. Jesus as presented here in his word and actions is the canon for testing if the operating spirit is the Holy Spirit. The Spirit "will not speak on his own authority, but whatever he hears he will speak"; "He will glorify me"; "He will take what is mine and declare it to you." As difficult as it is to apply such criteria in the life of the church, it is still comforting to know that the churches are not defenseless before those who proclaim in the name of the Spirit, "Lo, here" and "Lo, there."

As stated earlier, the remainder of this section so closely parallels 13:31–14:31 that nothing more need be said here. But perhaps in closing it would be helpful for the preacher to bring to an end the experience of this material by comment on the Evangelist's own way of concluding. According to vv. 29-30 the discourse was a success; it fulfilled its purpose. The disciples, so long confused, shout "Eureka!" They think Jesus has ceased to speak in figures and now speaks plainly. It is evident to the reader, however, that the difference is not in Jesus' speech; he has said the same words of promise, instruction and warning over and over in the same images and analogies. The difference is in their ears and in their minds.

The confession "we believe that you came from God" seals
this as true; they do understand and believe.

But the proof of discipleship does not rest in the final
analysis in the ears or in the mind or even on the lips. The
proof is in the life in the hour of testing, and that test they
were soon to fail. You will scatter, said Jesus; you will go
home and abandon me. Surely that word to the original disciples is here given as warning to the Johannine church in its
hour of trial. However, neither for the original followers nor
for those addressed by the Evangelist, and not for us who believe because of them is the final word a negative one. The
last word of the gospel is not a description of our weakness
and failure under pressure. The final word is as the first
word: it is about God. And so Jesus turns from a statement
about faltering discipleship and concludes with a word that
transcends all our success and our failure as his followers:
"In the world you have tribulation: but be of good cheer, I
have overcome the world" (v. 33).

The Farewell Prayer for His Disciples (17:1–26)

It is altogether proper to regard the prayer of 17:1–26 as
a part of the farewell discourses. While we are accustomed to
make sharp distinctions between addresses to the people
(sermon) and addresses to God (prayer), such is not the case
in the tradition in which the Gospel participates. Readers of
Old Testament Psalms are familiar with this pattern of interweaving words to the congregation and words to God. Or
perhaps a closer parallel to our present text is the farewell
speech of Moses in which Moses turns from the people and
addresses the heavens, blessing future generations of the
tribes of Israel (Deut 32–33). In the New Testament, Paul's
Epistle to the Romans offers frequent occasions of moving
easily from speaking to the readers to speaking to God. A
good example is 11:33–36. John 17:1–26 belongs to this
tradition.

We have already had occasion to note the sermonic nature of Jesus' prayers in this Gospel (11:42; 12:30). In view of
that, the listener to 17:1–26 should be ready to experience
this prayer from the position of one who overhears what
Jesus says to God in behalf of the church. In other words, the
readers are as a congregation during a pastoral prayer, not

directly addressed, but yet very much in the mind of the one who prays. The preacher who deals with this text could well consider using this same format and communication style for the sermon. The distance between a sermon and a pastoral prayer has become too great. After all, why should not a sermon be addressed to God as the primary audience? Good preaching is not solely *to* the people; good preaching is also *in behalf of* the people.

Let us now turn to the prayer itself; how are we to understand it? Its pre-passion setting in the Gospel would lead us to hear it as a prayer of the historical Jesus just prior to his glorification. This perspective is confirmed by v. 13: "But now I am coming to thee." However, the content of the prayer is very much that of an already glorified Christ looking down pastorally on his church on earth. This perspective is supported by v. 11: "And now I am no more in the world." What, then, is to be concluded? The prayer hangs between earth and heaven, between the pre- and post-resurrection moments of the Savior's sojourn. It is presented as a prayer of the historical Jesus, but not confined to that; it is a prayer of the glorified Christ, but not discontinuous with Jesus of Nazareth. In other words, the perspective of this prayer is no different from that of the remainder of the Gospel.

As to its structure, the prayer has been variously analyzed, as the commentaries will reflect. All, however, will agree to its stylized form and its poetic qualities. It is not unlike the Prologue in that regard. As the Prologue sang the pre-incarnation work of the Word, so 17:1–26 proclaims the post-incarnation ministry of the Word, Jesus Christ. Fortunately, in neither case is the message of the text contingent upon a unanimous scholarly opinion as to how to subdivide the passage into strophes. For our purpose here, the prayer will be discussed in view of its threefold content: Jesus' own return to glory (vv. 1–5), intercession for the disciples (vv. 6–19) and intercession for the readers of the Gospel who are disciples at least once removed (vv. 20–26). And the minister who has overcome the reluctance to preach (public) on a prayer (private) by observing in this Gospel the proclamatory nature of prayers and the petitionary nature of sermons, will find the chapter both significant and appropriate for the pulpit.

The first movement of the prayer (vv. 1–5) makes four clear announcements to the community of faith. First, since Christ is from God and returns to God, it follows that his primary benefaction to us is the revelation of God. Humanity is not left to its own devices of mind or imagination of the heart before the fundamental and universal questions of life's whence, whither and why. However one may interpret the particular acts of Jesus' ministry, crucifixion and resurrection, his coming among us as Word from God was the central demonstration that "God so loved the world." Second, the proper response to the revelation is not to devote oneself to precise and accurate formulation of the divinity of Christ which can, in fact, confuse faith's understanding of Christ as a revelation *of God.* Rather, the point of the Savior's sojourn is fulfilled in us when we know God through faith in the one God sent (v. 3). Third, because the world is the object of God's love and because it is to the world the revelation has come, the life-giving knowledge of God is available to all. To be sure, the Fourth Gospel both implies and states openly that there are insiders and outsiders in relation to the revealed Word. But one's place inside or outside is not determined by some Gnostic-like elitism, or the predisposition of one's soul, or the fixed will of God to exclude some in order to showcase divine sovereignty. One's being in light or darkness, possessing life or death is due to the decision precipitated by the coming of the Word which has created the crisis (judgment) of the world. Of course, as we have previously observed with this Evangelist (and it is true of other writers as well) theological reflections upon the fact that some accept and some reject the Gospel understand both the acceptance and the rejection within the overall will of God. But this perspective cannot legitimately be projected *in advance* upon any audience with the grim prediction that some of them cannot hear and believe. Even two thousand years of evidence that only a few truly hear the Word is no justification for the pulpit lowering its voice to a whisper so that only a few *can* hear the Word. If fifty said No and one said Yes yesterday, that ratio is not to be built into tomorrow's strategy. The church faces tomorrow with the faith and hope that all will see and hear. John 3:16 is God's Yes to the world; if there is a No, the world will have to say it.

The fourth and final announcement of 17:1–5 is that the return of Christ to God does not end his ministry to his followers. The ministry of the glorified Christ continues endlessly. For him to ask God to restore him to the former glory is in no sense a selfish prayer, for in the presence of God Christ will petition for the Church that prayers be answered, that the Spirit be sent to guide, instruct and remind, and that in the form of the Spirit Christ continues as counselor and comforter. In this sense, therefore, the prayer of Christ for a return to glory is really as much a prayer for the disciples as is the remainder of the chapter. The farewell discourse has already said as much: "Nevertheless I tell you the truth; it is to your advantage that I go away, for if I do not go away, the Counselor will not come to you; but if I go, I will send him to you" (16:7).

Since vv. 1–5 deal with the departure of Jesus to the presence of God, one would expect the next section to take up again the subject of the coming of the Spirit to be with the church. Such, however, is not the case. Instead, the attention in vv. 6–19 is upon those original disciples to whom Jesus had entrusted the word of truth. Why elaborate on Jesus' prayer for the apostles who, by the time of this Gospel, are all dead? The reason comes clear with a little reflection. In chaps. 14–16 the tie between the glorified Christ and the Johannine church, the continuity between the departed Christ and the readers, was the Paraclete, the Holy Spirit, sent in Jesus' stead. The anxiety of the readers was repeatedly addressed with the assuring words that the Spirit would not lead them in a different direction but would teach of Jesus, remind of Jesus, glorify Jesus, witness to Jesus. But, assuring as that may have been, was there any clear and certain line of continuity between the glorified Christ and the church of the readers? At the mouth of two witnesses a thing is established. Was there a second witness to confirm that the Johannine church was a community abiding in the truth? The answer was a clear Yes. Between the glorified Christ and the church were two bonds: the Spirit Christ sent, and the apostles to whom he gave the word and sent into the world. In other words, the Johannine church is assured of being both inspired and apostolic.

Such, then, is the function of vv. 6–19: in the form of a

prayer for the original disciples, Jesus establishes for the readers the clear and certain apostolic connection. If there were any question (and there must have been) whether the word of Jesus had been transmitted in purity to a later generation of believers, the sentences of 17:6–19 serve as bonds of steel. Between Jesus and the church were the apostles and these apostles were given of God to Jesus (v. 6); Christ had given to them the word of God (vv. 6–8); they had received that word, believed it and kept it (vv. 6–8); they had not been corrupted by the unbelieving world for they were not of the world and, in fact, the world hated them as it had Jesus (vv. 9–16); even though one of the apostles had gone astray, even that was within God's knowledge and according to Scripture (v. 12); just as Jesus had sanctified himself in total dedication to God, so were the apostles set apart (consecrated) for the truth (vv. 17–19); and the apostles had as their sole purpose in life the continuation of that mission which Jesus had from God (v. 18). The Evangelist would leave no one in doubt: the church is not an orphan in the world, a thing dislodged, a progeny of uncertain parentage, an accident of history, the frightened child of huddled rumors and superstitions. The pedigree of truth (as though truth needed to show its credentials) is beyond question: from God to Christ to the apostles to the church.

The prayer concludes with a petition for those who come to faith through the apostolic witness (vv. 20–26). Here the writer's awareness of the reader, a characteristic of the entire Gospel, again becomes pronounced. Every generation of believers can read vv. 20–26 and be assured that the prayer of Jesus is in their behalf. This paragraph erases all distinctions between believers of the first, or second, third or subsequent generations; there are only believers. And all believers have come to be such in the same way: through the word.

The prayer for all future disciples has as its central petition the unity of all believers, a unity that is informed and empowered by the unity of God and Christ (vv. 20–23). Because God and Christ were one, the revelation of truth in no way suffered from uncertainty nor was it blurred by confusion. So must it be among Christ's followers and between those followers and Christ. When this is so, the witness to the truth about God will continue to be made effectively to the world. Confusion and division must not disrupt or corrupt the unceasing witness to the Creator who gave life and light and grace to all who believe the word.

It is appropriate, then, to use 17:20–26 in the context of ecumenical discussions and efforts for Christian unity. In so doing care must be taken to make it clear that the prayer was not originally concerned with the smooth meshing of the gears of denominational machinery. But given the fact of denominationalism, this prayer can inspire unity conversation with the vision of a harmony among believers after the manner of that between Christ and God and between Christ and his followers. Secondly, this prayer for the oneness of believers can inform ecumenical discussions as to the true and proper ground of unity: trust in God through the revelation in Jesus Christ. For example, no unity should be sought on a racial or ethnic basis, for the Evangelist has already said repeatedly that other sheep will be brought who are not of this fold (10:16) and other nations will be included along with those in Israel who believe (11:52). And finally, this prayer can function as a judgment upon lesser forms of unity that arise out of political expediency, mutual accommodation to error, and belief at the level of the lowest common denominator.

The prayer closes with the two-fold pattern of promise with which we have now grown familiar. As in 14:2–3, Christ desires that all his disciples may be with him forever in glory. But the church is not asked to survive on that promise for the future. The striking contribution of this Gospel for the life and encouragement of believers is the word of Christ "in the meantime." Here as in 14:23 and elsewhere, the assurance for the interim is the abiding love of God and the presence of Christ in their midst (v. 26). The church of every generation and every place which believes this word will not simply survive but will do so with a flourish.

A closing note to the preacher: the degree of effectiveness of a message on 17:20–26 will depend in large measure upon enabling the listeners to sense that they are being prayed for. To hear one's name spoken in a prayer is a powerful and moving experience. Pause to illustrate or demonstrate so that the church will sense what it means for Christ to be praying for them. Ministers of sensitivity may well frame the sermon on these verses as a prayer rather than as an exhortation, thrashing the listener with *ought, must* and *should*.

The Farewell
(John 18:1–20:31)

It is a matter of general scholarly agreement that the block of tradition we call the "passion narrative" was fixed rather early in the preaching and teaching of the church. Gospels that differ with each other rather widely elsewhere move closer together in this section, perhaps testifying to the centrality of this material for the life of the church regardless of its local setting and particular needs. But even so, the Johannine fingerprints will not be missing from this section. That fact, however, is in no way to be taken as disrespect by this Evangelist for the inner sanctum of the Gospels. On the contrary, fundamental convictions about Christology, the meaning of Jesus' death, and the relation of the risen Christ to his church make it essential that these perspectives be carried through to the very last line.

Preaching that is based not simply on the passion narrative but the passion narrative *according to John* will pay close attention to this Evangelist's telling of the story. The comments which follow will seek to do just that.

Arrest (18:1–12)

Nothing of sighing or beating the breast, nothing of sorrow unto death, nothing of sweating as it were drops of blood, nothing of agonizing before the will of God is to be found in this Evangelist's account of the night of the arrest. The name "Gethsemane" which has, because of the Synoptics, become a synonym for anguished prayer, is here replaced by the single description, "a garden" (v. 1). The writer has drained from the account almost every drop of emotion. He has spared us the treacherous kiss of Judas (Mark 14:44–45). Judas is there, to be sure, but he simply stands there (v. 5). The act of betrayal consisted of bringing the arresting officers to the secluded garden which Judas knew so well, having been there often with Jesus and the other disciples (v. 2). That we have here a night scene, quite early preserved in the tradition (1 Cor 11:23) and already said dramatically by this Evangelist (13:30), is even more vivid in the phrase "lanterns and torches" (v. 3). In addition to Judas, the other disciple singled out is Simon Peter whose effort to defend Jesus is mentioned in all four Gospels. That this writer alone gives the name of the servant (v. 10) whose ear (literally, earlobe) was cut off is an intriguing detail. We have had many occasions to observe this Evangelist's penchant for inserting specifics as to times, places, persons and even distances. Commentaries disagree with each other in accounting for this. Some refer to the writer's source, others to the tendency of stories to increase in details with repetition and passing time, while others see in these literary touches an argument for historicity in an otherwise noticeably theological treatment of Jesus' life and ministry.

The preacher will want to notice especially the size and broadly representative nature of the arresting crowd. A "band of soldiers" (vv. 3, 12) was a "cohort," a Roman army unit of 600 men. A "captain" ("chiliarch," v. 12) was literally an officer over 1000 men. However loosely one translates the terms, this Gospel fills the garden with soldiers. More strikingly, all of Judaism is involved in the arrest and seizure of Jesus. Officers of the chief priests (Sadducees) and Pharisees (v. 3) are present, thus implicating the entire official leadership of the Jews. Even more striking is the presence of Roman soldiers (vv. 3, 12) in the garden. This Gospel alone implicates Rome in the arrest of Jesus even though some commentaries understand that both Matthew (27:11) and Mark (15:2) imply such by the fact of Pilate's knowledge, without asking, of the accusations against Jesus. Whether this Evangelist had an historical source unavailable to or unused by the others or is here reflecting theologically upon the arrest of Jesus, the point is clear: the unbelieving world joins forces against the Word from God, seeking to silence that Word by violent death.

Were the scene enacted on a stage, Jesus would be at the center, not a victim of betrayal and seizure, but easily the dominant figure controlling all the action. Judas carries out the charge given him at the last supper (13:27) and then just stands there. Peter courageously tries to defend his friend in what appears to be an impossible situation, only to discover that his friend needs no defending at all. Soldiers and of-

ficers, armed and ready, cannot act until they receive their
orders, not from emperor or governor but from Jesus himself: "I told you I am he; so, if you seek me, let these men go"
(v. 8). Until Jesus permits it they can do nothing but fall to
the ground at the sound of the divine "I am" (vv. 5-6). The
Jesus of this scene is as we have met throughout the Gospel.
His question, "Whom do you seek?" is almost exactly the
question of 1:38 which was the first utterance of Jesus in this
Gospel. Because his hour has come, those who could not arrest him before (7:30, 44; 8:20, 59; 10:39; 12:36) may now do
so. Jesus had said no one would take his life, he would give it
(10:18), and so he does. Whatever struggle with death Jesus
experienced (chaps. 11, 12) that is over now: "shall I not
drink the cup which the Father has given me?" (v. 11).

Some preachers may tend to avoid this account of the
garden scene as lacking in the realities of treason and late
night arrest. If sermons are to be true to life, would it not be
better to turn to the blood, sweat and tears of the Synoptic
Gethsemane? Perhaps, but before doing so, one should ponder carefully v. 9: "This was to fulfill the word which he had
spoken, 'Of those whom thou gavest me I lost not one.' "Here
a reference to something Jesus had said earlier (6:39; 17:12)
is treated almost as a word of Scripture, a prophecy being
fulfilled. What does this mean? It means that from the writer's perspective the scenes before us now are seen as sufficiently past as to be understood in broad reflection, as one
would look at the Old Testament and see promise and fulfillment from a Christian perspective. What Jesus said and did
is now "the Christian tradition." It is not intended, then, that
the reader experience being taken back into the garden to
feel and see and hear afresh that awful night. Rather, the
reader is told to stay where he or she is and look back upon it
with the advantages distance provides. Is that an unreal perspective? Certainly not. While there is much truth conveyed
in the expression "You had to be there," it is also the case
that those not there can see the broader picture, trace devel-
opments, perceive lines of meaning, and in general work
with the insights that come only in reflection. Many of us
who "have been there" on occasions of extreme loss, grief
and wrenching suffering have said with the wisdom that
comes later, "I see now what I did not see at the time." This

Evangelist reminds us that it is sometimes helpful to preach from a distance.

Interrogation by Religious Leaders (18:13–27)

Commentaries which seek to reconstruct the trial of Jesus before Jewish authorities rely most heavily on the Synoptics, fitting into that framework the appearance before Annas, the account of which is found only in the text before us. That reconstruction usually consists of Jesus being questioned the evening of the arrest in the home of the high priest (only Matt 26:57 gives the name Caiaphas) in the presence of priests, scribes, and elders, an early morning meeting of the Sanhedrin before which Jesus is charged with blasphemy, Jesus being subjected to indignities (Matt 26:67; Mark 14:65; Luke 22:63–64), and then delivering Jesus to Pilate. In the Fourth Gospel, the only official action by the Jews is the questioning before Annas. Caiaphas "who was high priest that year" (v. 13) is mentioned in this section four times but there is no description of any action by him or before him. Perhaps the reason is that Caiaphas, along with the Sanhedrin, had already determined without trial or even a hearing, that Jesus must die (v. 14; 11:49–51).

Historians have been baffled by this Evangelist's focus upon Annas, Caiaphas' father-in-law. Responses have ranged from accepting the account as being drawn from solid sources available to this writer to discounting it all as further proof that this Gospel provides little reliable historical data. Is there not another way to understand the Evangelist's references to both Annas (vv. 15, 16, 19, 22) and Caiaphas (vv. 13, 24) as high priest when, in fact, there could be but one? Irony and even sarcasm, already seen repeatedly in this Gospel, may be the writer's way of removing any significance from the role of the Jewish authorities in the glorification of the Son. The reader is provided some sad comedy in the scene. Since the high priesthood was for life, maybe Caiaphas, "high priest *that* year" was a Roman appointee. He certainly had acted and decided against Jesus on political grounds (v. 14). And perhaps Annas was the true high priest who now has no power but who still goes through an empty ritual. He asks in general about Jesus' disciples and his teaching but not about Jesus' words or signs which could be used to support a charge of blasphemy. In other words, there was nothing worth reporting, says the Evangelist. Jesus was slapped by an attendant (v. 22) and sent to Caiaphas.

What, then, did the writer regard as worth reporting in any detail? Obviously the three-fold denial by Peter. Of the 31 lines in this section, 16 are about Peter. Details such as describing the maid as the one who kept the door, and the fire made with charcoal, and a servant who was a kinsman of the one whose ear Peter had cut off, made it clear where the Evangelist's interest lies. The trial receives little ink; after all, Jesus has already said the hour of his glorification is here and that he will give his life, no one will take it. Rather the Evangelist, ever conscious of the reader and the church, offers a dramatic contrast in these sketches: inside, Jesus is being questioned; outside, Peter is being questioned; inside, Jesus stands firm in all that he had taught; outside, Peter denies everything he ever said. The fact is, the trial of Jesus has been over ever since Jesus prayed, "Father, glorify thy name" (12:18). But the trial of Peter, and of the disciples, and of the Johannine community, and of the church today, is not over; it continues. Again, the Evangelist proves himself more preacher than historian.

(Let the interpreter hold in mind the presence of "another disciple" in this story. Beginning in 13:23–25, the portrait of Peter hangs beside that of another disciple whose name is withheld but whose place and qualities overshadow those of Peter. At a later point these two will be considered in more detail.)

Interrogation by Pontius Pilate (18:28–19:16)

In the Synoptics, Jesus' trial before Pontius Pilate consists of three brief episodes: Jesus is silent before Pilate's questioning; Pilate offers to release Jesus instead of Barabbas; at the crowd's insistence, Pilate delivers Jesus for crucifixion. Luke interrupts this order with a brief appearance before Herod Antipas (23:6–12). In the Fourth Gospel, however, the account is quite lengthy, consisting of seven episodes, with the scenes alternating between the inside of the praetorium where Pilate questions Jesus, and the outside where Pilate deals with the Jewish authorities. The account has three dramatic foci: Jesus, clear and strong and obviously in control of the entire proceeding; Pilate the Roman governor, shuttling back and forth seven times between Jesus and the Jews, reduced in role to a kind of fearful, frustrated, indecisive lieutenant; the Jews, the epitome of "the world" in this Gospel, operating solely on appearance, with murder in their hearts but unwilling to enter a Gentile building lest they be ceremonially defiled (v. 28).

Episode One: Pilate outside trying to ascertain the charge against Jesus, willing to let the Jews handle it, but has to take the case since it involves a capital offense (vv. 29-32).

Episode Two: Pilate inside, quizzing Jesus about the nature of kingship and truth, resorting to philosophy and sarcasm before a revelation he cannot grasp (vv. 33-38).

Episode Three: Pilate outside, declaring Jesus not guilty and offering to release him according to a custom at Passover. The Jews ask for the bandit Barabbas (vv. 38-40).

Episode Four: Pilate inside, subjecting Jesus to scourging and mockery (19:1-3).

Episode Five: Pilate outside, displaying the mocked and beaten Jesus, thinking thereby to satisfy the Jewish authorities but without success (vv. 4-7).

Episode Six: Pilate inside before Jesus, now more fearful and therefore more bullying, claiming power of life and death over Jesus. Jesus tells Pilate his power has been granted from above (vv. 8-11).

Episode Seven: Pilate outside before the Jews in one final effort to release Jesus, now sits officially in the seat of judgment and pressures the Jews into confessing Caesar is their king (vv. 12-16).

The dramatic skill of this Evangelist is most impressive and the preacher will want to convey that quality in the sermon so that the text can affect as well as inform the listener. But the drama has its message and the Johannine church surely was not only encouraged by it but also found in it cause for celebration. After all, in the person of Jesus, the church saw itself, charged but not guilty, oppressed but not submissive, mocked but not ashamed, under attack by both civil and religious authority but holding firm to the truth, being killed but confident of membership in the kingdom where God's will prevails even in ugly injustices.

The preacher of this text may decide that the listeners today need to have the encouragement and support that comes from identification with Jesus over against the forces of political or religious oppression. In parts of the world Christians do now stand where Jesus stood and in such cases, presenting the message from this perspective and permitting this identification would be most appropriate. But it is encumbent upon the preacher to ask whether recent history and current conditions do not demand that the sermon effect listener identification with the religious leaders outside Pilate's hall. In such case, the text is an indictment, for here is the portrait of religion that has lost its soul by compromise thinly veiled by empty ritual and false patriotism. The indictment is three-fold. First, there is careful attention to ceremonial purity while demanding death to one who is a threat to position, income and security. One is reminded of the celebrated case of the felon serving a sentence in a federal prison who refused to sing in the prison choir because he held membership in a denomination that opposed singing to the accompaniment of instrumental music. Second, the claim of concern for the people and nation is emptied of meaning by the request to release upon the public a known bandit. Such inequities reveal the hypocrisy in some religious endorsements of law and order. And finally, religion here denies its faith and announces its real creed: Caesar is king. In other words, the state with all its way of shaping and controlling the economic, political, social, and domestic and personal definition of who we are and how we live is acknowledged as the supreme power. Of course, there will be in a few hours the rites at the Temple in which God is invoked, but here before the Roman praetorium religion is making its confession of faith. And at Passover, too; on the anniversary of freedom from the pharaoh, the pharaoh is embraced.

The other place from which to hear and speak this text is the praetorium, the center of governmental process. Unaware that his role in this drama is by God's permission (19:11), Pilate claims authority but gradually succumbs to confusion and fear, in the end abdicating all power and submitting to the hatred and prejudices of petty local leaders. His running back and forth between Jesus and the Jews is tragi-comical, dramatizing the immobilizing force of indecision. Shuttling between private judgment and public pressure, the governor abandons the state's responsibility in matters of guilt or innocence. His only victory in the case is his success in getting the chief priests, already dressed for the holy day services, to confess, "Caesar is king." While it is the general tendency of the Gospels to place less blame for Jesus' death upon Rome than upon the Jews, one cannot regard this account as a "whitewashing" of Pilate. This Evangelist has understood Rome's responsible involvement from the night of the arrest (18:12). But the portrayal of Pilate is so realistic that many have identified with both his problem and his failure. Such identification is not confined to those in positions of power. None of us is exempt from decisions hammered out under extreme pressure, decisions which demand of us not only wisdom and insight but penitence and moral courage.

Crucifixion (19:17–30)

In telling the story of Jesus of Nazareth, the church has tended to blur distinctions among the various Gospel records and to offer the narrative as a single account. This has been especially true of stories of the birth, resurrection appearances and the crucifixion. For example, it has long been popular for pulpits to give attention prior to Easter to "The Seven Words from the Cross." For whatever values there are in such treatments, there are lost the special messages and insights each Evangelist brings to the reader. The preacher would do well, then, to listen carefully to the text before us lest its message be absorbed and lost under the general topic of Jesus' death.

One notices first of all the brevity of the story in John 19:17–30, shorter by far than even Mark's account. Here there are no multitudes following, no passersby, no taunts nor mocking, no conversations with the two thieves, no darkness, no earthquakes, no indication of how long Jesus was on the cross, no emptying of tombs, and no splitting of the temple veil. This Evangelist writes with such restraint that no one could get the impression that the efficacy of the cross is its power to pull sorrow and tears from the reader. Squeezing melancholy from the scene should be avoided by the preacher. It is also quite obvious that the passion materials in this Gospel contain much more frequent references to ful-

filling Scripture than in earlier signs and speeches. This may
be because pertinent Old Testament texts were already imbedded in the pre-Johannine tradition. However, the reason
may lie in the writer's theological emphasis: Jesus in his
death brings to fulfillment and conclusion the rituals and
regulations of Judaism. This perspective is evident not only
in the action of the soldiers (v. 24) and in Jesus' words, "I
thirst" (v. 29), but especially in the description of the treatment of the corpse (vv. 31–37).

Whatever may have been contained in the tradition
available to this Evangelist, it is evident that in his hands the
account is carefully controlled theologically. Apparently the
intention was in no sense to distort history but to aid the
reader to understand the meaning of the event. The theological themes developed are basically two, which have appeared earlier in the Gospel and now govern the writer's
understanding of Jesus' crucifixion. Either one or both could
be most suggestive and fruitful for sermons on this text. One
theme or motif is that which earlier clustered around the image of the Good Shepherd (10:11–18). A good shepherd gives
his life for the sheep, caring for them to the very end. Jesus
gives his life; it is not taken from him. The text before us follows that thesis in every detail. Because he is, on his own,
laying down his life, Jesus carries his own cross (Simon of
Cyrene of the Synoptics does not appear here), does not
scream out the cry of dereliction, says "I thirst" only to fulfill
the Scripture, and in the act of death, bows his head and
gives up his spirit, the picture of serene self-giving. Even the
act of giving his mother and the beloved disciple into each
other's care is not described so as to wrench the reader's
heart. Rather the Good Shepherd cares and provides for his
own. If the Johannine community knew of a special relationship between Mary and the beloved disciple, they now understood it to have been authorized and blessed by Jesus in the
hour of death. And to die with the words, "It is finished,"
must here mean much more than "My life is ended." The expression is better understood as the Son's obedient comple-
tion of the demands of "the hour" of death, just as he had
earlier concluded his public ministry with the words, "I glorified thee on earth, having accomplished the work which
thou gavest me to do" (17:4).

The second theological theme is that of kingship. The charge against Jesus was that he falsely claimed to be a king. All of Pilate's interrogation focused upon this issue, and it was finally the Jew's insistence that only Caesar is king which pressured Pilate to act against Jesus. The mockery of Jesus by the soldiers who provided a royal robe, a crown of thorns and empty, sarcastic praise played upon the expression, "King of the Jews." This is the title Pilate posts on the cross, resisting attempts by Jewish authorities to replace the title with a statement to the effect that Jesus *claimed* the title. And the announcement is to the whole world, being written in the languages enabling everyone to read, Hebrew, Latin and Greek. The Roman governor has said it as a universal truth, "Jesus of Nazareth, the King of the Jews." And the irony of it is unavoidable: beyond Pilate's stubborn sarcasm lies the truth of what he wrote. But beyond that irony is a greater one: those who had insisted that the imposter be crucified unwittingly have enthroned him. " 'And I, when I am lifted up from the earth, will draw all men to myself.' He said this to show by what death he was to die" (12:32–33). The crucifixion of Jesus is the lifting up of Jesus which, in its fuller sense, is the glorifying of the Son. Enthroned by execution; glorified by his executioners; returned to the presence of God by those who would put him out of their sight: this is the message the Evangelist wants the church to hear. There exists nowhere a stronger, nor stranger, affirmation of the sovereignty of God in human affairs.

Burial (19:31–42)

For the handling of the corpse and the burial to receive almost as much attention as the crucifixion itself is enough to draw the attention to any reader. That such a detailed account of the disposition of Jesus' body had as its primary purpose a polemic against those Christian spiritualists (Gnostics?) whose Christology had no place for the physical is a real possibility. Heretics who denied Jesus Christ came in the flesh were certainly known in the Johannine community (1 John 4:2–3). The burial of Jesus, which one would normally assume following death, came to be explicitly stated in Christian confessions, both early (1 Cor 15:4) and officially (Apostles Creed). Perhaps proof of real physical death and

proof of resurrection of the body were issues at stake in all
these accounts. Of the two stories about Jesus' body in the
text before us (vv. 31–37; 38–42), the former certainly involves a polemic, or at least an argument. Such is the thrust
of v. 35: "He who saw it has borne witness—his testimony is
true, and he knows that he tells the truth—that you also may
believe." With whom and about what does the writer thus
argue?

The account begins with the Jews' request that Pilate
honor the Passover Sabbath by removing the bodies before
sunset. The request is granted by administering the Roman
death torture. By breaking the legs, death was hastened but
pain was intensified. With the dramatic touch of the story-
teller, the Evangelist relates last what happened to Jesus
even though Jesus was in the middle and reasonably would
have been second in line for the torture. Apparently Jesus
was already dead (he gave his life), but the spear thrust was
to make sure. Out came blood and water. At this point the
Evangelist interrupts the narration to call attention to the
fact of eye-witness evidence, to the absolute truth of the witness, and to the faith-enabling value of that testimony. What
truth is at stake here?

That the Evangelist is speaking symbolically in this text
is evident, but symbolism can break loose into unrestrained
allegory. The commentaries recall many of the fascinating
but fanciful interpretations of the "blood and water." For example, out of the side of the second Adam came the cure for
the sins that followed from the creation of Eve from the side
of the first Adam. Of the many lines of interpretation possible, two seem most congenial to the context and to Johannine theology. The first is actually stated in the text: these
events fulfilled Scripture. Of particular importance is the application of the law concerning the slaughter of the Passover
lamb: its bones are not to be broken (Exod 12:46; Num 9:12).
We have already noted (chap. 13) that in the Fourth Gospel
Jesus does not eat the Passover, he *is* the Passover. The time
is right: the afternoon of the day of Preparation (v. 31). The
method is right: draining the lamb's blood but not breaking
any bones. Even the earlier reference to hyssop (v. 29) which
was used in the Passover ritual (Exod 12:2) may have been
intended to nourish this interpretation of Jesus' death. By

this symbolism the Evangelist has not only announced the Passover which ends all Passovers and the death which renders useless further sacrificial deaths, but also he has proclaimed a new exodus which Passover commemorates. This new exodus is not from the slavery of Egypt but from the bondage of sin and death (chap. 8). To the liberation of God's world the writer has witnessed and the preacher of this text could do no better than continue that witness.

The second line of interpretation appropriate to the whole of this Gospel lies in the view of blood and water here as symbols of the eucharist and baptism. Baptismal and eucharistic language abounds throughout this Gospel and therefore make a sacramental interpretation of 19:31–37 quite possible. Both baptism and the eucharist are directly tied to Jesus and have their meaning through the believer's participation in him. Now that Jesus is dead, the sacraments of the church have their full significance and efficacy. And it probably is not inappropriate for the preacher to support this interpretation with the kindred statement from 1 John 5:6–8: "This is he who came by water and blood, Jesus Christ, not with the water only but with the water and the blood. And the Spirit is the witness, because the Spirit is the truth. There are three witnesses, the Spirit, the water, and the blood; and these three agree."

Whether the preacher develops the message of 19:31–42 along the line of the Passover or the Christian sacraments, or both, two matters need to be remembered. One, these lines of interpretation are really not independent of each other. All four Gospels relate baptism and the eucharist to the Exodus and to the Passover. Two, in both interpretations Jesus continues to minister to his church after death. That the ministry of Jesus continued beyond his death is most important in this Gospel. It is not incidental, then, that the account concerning the corpse of Christ is told so as to remind the reader of the body of Christ.

As for vv. 38–42, it is difficult to know if this functions solely as a conclusion to the crucifixion story. After all, there needs to be closure to questions as to what happened to the body, who prepared it, and where it was entombed. If so, then the conclusion to the one episode serves as introduction to the next: the empty tomb. There are, of course, differences here with the Synoptics as to who prepared the body, Joseph and Nicodemus or the women, and when, the day of Preparation (Friday) or the first day of the week (Sunday), or at least the women so intended. The commentaries differ as to whether the two accounts can or need be harmonized. It seems important to this Evangelist that two disciples who had been secretive, fearful and very private in their relation to Jesus, now act openly, courageously and at great expense. Cynics read the paragraph and observe that many sponsors arrive on the scene after the battle is over. Disciples, not caretakers, are the need of the hour. More generous readers find occasion here to celebrate. In his death, they say, Jesus continues to draw to himself persons who had formerly been hesitant and unbelieving. Had Jesus not said as much when speaking of the cross: in death I will draw all people to myself?

Resurrection (20:1–29)

Trite as it may seem, we need to remind ourselves that the New Testament offers no account of the resurrection of Jesus. What we do have are reports about the empty tomb and appearances of the risen Christ. Although showing some kinship with each other, the various records seem to reflect different sources and certainly make their own emphases. The two major divergences are in Mark 16:1–8, in which there is no resurrection appearance, and in 1 Cor 15:3–8, in which there is no appearance to a woman.

The resurrection materials in the Fourth Gospel constitute a carefully constructed piece of literature consisting of two separate stories (20:1–18; 19–29), each with two parts. All four episodes are said to have occurred on Sunday and may have once existed as separate stories used in Christian worship. As the Evangelist has composed the narrative, each of the two principal stories describes scenes involving some of the original disciples. Then each story centers upon an individual's experience of the risen Lord, in the first case Mary Magdalene and in the second, Thomas. After showing how each came to recognize Jesus, the narrator turns again to a larger audience, Mary Magdalene going to tell the disciples, and Jesus turning from Thomas to pronounce a blessing on all those who have not seen and yet believe (v. 29).

Before remarking upon the two stories, the preacher and the whole church need to notice how restrained were the uses of resurrection stories in the New Testament. Unlike some post-New Testament accounts which sought to shock and coerce faith by having the risen Christ appear to passersby and the general unbelieving public, within the canon Christ appeared to believers. The church witnessed to the resurrection of Christ but the resurrection was not a faith-compelling wonder which overwhelmed the disinterested. According to Acts 2:22–32, Simon Peter referred to the life and work of Jesus as *known to all* (v. 22), but as to God raising Jesus from the dead, "of that *we* are all witnesses" (v. 32). Easter vindicates the faith of those who are followers of Jesus.

Appearance to Mary Magdalene (20:1–18)

As stated above this story is actually the interweaving of two episodes, that of Peter and the beloved disciple and that of Mary Magdalene. In both episodes, faith in Christ's resurrection is generated, but in different ways. In the case of Peter and the beloved disciple, as we have now come to expect (13:22–25; 18:15–16), the beloved disciple wins the race to the tomb. Peter brashly enters first, looks about, sees everything and nothing, and leaves. The beloved disciple enters, looks upon the same scene, and believes. Even though they did not yet understand the Scriptures concerning the resurrection (v. 9), the beloved disciple becomes the first believer in Christ's resurrection. And upon what evidence? The very least: an empty tomb containing grave cloths. Without seeing and without hearing, this closest of all the disciples believes. Such a relationship apparently does not need the scaffolding of sight and sound.

Mary Magdalene, on the other hand, represents faith being formed another way. The empty tomb did not even hint resurrection for her; it only saddened her with the assumption that Jesus' body had been stolen. So far from such faith is she that the appearance of two angels (v. 12) does not break her sorrow. Even the voice of Jesus does not at first stir faith in her. In fact, when first she saw him, she did not recognize Jesus (v. 14). Unlike some current popular religionists, Mary Magdalene was a follower of Jesus but she certainly was not out looking for a miracle. Only when he spoke her name (he

knows his own and calls them by name, and they know his
voice, 10:3–4) did she believe (v. 16). Unlike the beloved disciple, Mary Magdalene comes to faith through the word of
Christ, and by that word she must be sustained, for she cannot
act as though life is now as it was before the crucifixion. This
is Jesus before her, to be sure; the risen Christ is none other
than the crucified Jesus. But even so, things are different now.
The ministry of the historical Jesus is over; now begins the
ministry of the glorified and ascended Christ. Mary Magdalene cannot resume the old relationship with her Lord, for
Christ now relates to his followers by giving them the Paraclete, the Spirit. Therefore Jesus says to her, "Do not hold me"
(v. 17). She and the disciples and the church today are not to
long for the way it was, as though that time were a brief Camelot. Rather they, and we, are to believe his word: it is best for
you that I go away; if I do not go away, the Spirit will not
come; the Spirit will remain with you forever; greater works
than I have done, you will do because I go to my Father.

Appearance to His Disciples (20:19–29)

If the Beloved Disciple believed without evidence except
an empty tomb, and Mary Magdalene believed because of a
word, the disciples (without Thomas) believed because they
saw him. "When he had said this, he showed them his hands
and his side. Then the disciples were glad when they saw the
Lord" (v. 20). But for the absent Thomas, neither the word of
witness nor sight of Jesus would be sufficient: his faith could
be sure only after physical contact (v. 25). The spectrum of
faith in the risen Christ is now complete; the beloved disciple
alone has that ideal faith which needs no proof, Mary Magdalene believes in response to a word, the disciples see and believe, while Thomas must touch in order to trust. Whether
Thomas ever actually touched Jesus is not clear (vv. 27–29),
but what is clear is that faith is not for all the same experience, neither is it generated for all with the same kind and
degree of "evidence." For some, faith is born and grows as
quietly as a child sleeping on grandmother's lap. For others,
faith is a lifetime of wrestling with the angel. Some cannot
remember when they did not believe, while others cannot remember anything else, their lives having been shattered and
reshaped by the decision of faith.

Given these varieties of faith experiences, it is most important to observe that not one of the four episodes is made normative for everyone. What the Evangelist does insist upon is that the possibility for faith is not limited to that circle of original disciples nor to their experiences of Christ. In fact, Christ pronounces a blessing upon all who have not seen and yet who believe (v. 29). This is to affirm that faith is available to all persons in all places without any diminution of value or efficacy by reason of distance of time or place from the time and place of Jesus of Nazareth.

This assurance needs to be heard by the church over and over again, and by preachers in particular, for that which makes faith possible is the word of Christian witness, beginning with the apostles and continuing until now. That this was Jesus' vision of his work continuing was voiced earlier in the farewell prayer: "I do not pray for these only, but also for those who are to believe in me through their word" (17:20). The church and the pulpit need to feel the weight of importance here placed upon the word, a weight not unlike the "burden" of the prophet. A few years ago the most common criticism of preaching was that sermons were not biblical. Where justified, the criticism was a serious indictment of preaching. More recently, however, the common criticism is that the sermons are offered as though nothing were at stake. Where justified, that criticism focuses upon a flaw that is not simply serious; it is fatal.

To equip his disciples for this work and for the difficulties that will beset it, the risen Lord gives to them the Holy Spirit. When he had breathed on them, he said, "Receive the Holy Spirit" (v. 22). This fulfills the promise made in the farewell discourses. Brief as it is, this act and statement by Christ is the Johannine Pentecost. Luke's Pentecost is lengthily and dramatically told, consisting of the promise of power, the forty days of appearances, ten days of prayer and waiting, and the outpouring of the Spirit with attendant signs and wonders (Acts 1:1–2:42). No such commentary surrounds this text. For an elaboration of what receiving the Holy Spirit meant in the Johannine community one needs to re-read chaps. 14–16. Here at 20:22 only one new dimension to the presence of the Spirit is provided: the apostles are granted the authority to pronounce or refuse to pronounce forgiveness of sin (v. 23; Matt 16:19; 18:18). Through the apostles the benefits of Christ as well as the mission of Christ are to continue in the world. Through the Holy Spirit the departed and ascended Christ always abides with his church.

Concluding Statement (20:30–31)

In the introduction to this volume this statement of the Evangelist's purpose was discussed at some length and that need not be repeated here. Those comments might, however, be more meaningful now that we have reflected on the Gospel together than when they were first read. If this concluding statement is used as a sermon text, the preacher will want to be sure the expression "that you may believe" is filled with Johannine understandings of faith as the Gospel itself has portrayed them. There is faith and then there is faith. There is faith based on signs and faith that needs none; there is faith weak and faith strong, faith shallow and faith deep, faith growing and faith retreating. Faith is not in this Gospel a decision once and for all, but a decision anew in every situation. This understanding of faith should enrich and enlarge the life of the believing community, especially where the conversion model has been so dominant. This is not to discount the paradigm of faith generally patterned after the conversion of Paul, but to remind ourselves of the alternatives no less valid.

THE EPILOGUE TO THE GOSPEL
(JOHN 21:1-25)

To call 21:1-25 an epilogue is a literary and not a value judgment. This is to say that while it is clear that this chapter is not part of the main fabric of the Gospel it is also clear that this chapter is part of the received text and no less "Scripture" than chapters 1-20. Obviously 20:30-31 was written as a conclusion to what preceded it, and no less obviously, the phrase "after this" only loosely and vaguely joins 21:1-25 to that body of material. Many commentators take 21:24-25 as the signature of a later hand, perhaps a disciple of the Beloved Disciple or a disciple of the author of chapters 1-20. Of greater concern to us, however, than matters of authorship is the question of the purpose of the epilogue. Why was it added? If an author's intention is a factor in interpreting a text, then the issue of purpose is a concern for the preacher as well as the academician.

A number of judgments as to the reason for the epilogue are worthy of consideration, each of them having some support in the text itself. A popular position is that the material had as its primary aim the rehabilitation of Peter. Just as Peter denied Jesus three times he is given opportunity to affirm his love three times (vv. 15-19). The strength of this view is somewhat eroded, however, by the less than complimentary portrayal of Peter in comparison with the Beloved Disciple in the preceding (vv. 4-8) and succeeding (vv. 20-23) stories. No less widely accepted is the opinion that the point of the chapter is to clear up a church wide rumor that the Beloved Disciple was never to die. If, in fact, one of the disciples was alive long after the others were dead, that could generate a story of endless life being granted to him, especially if he were the disciple closest to Jesus. While the epilogue does clear up the origin of such a misunderstanding (vv. 22-23), there is too much other material in the chapter to justify this as the sole purpose of the writer. The same can be said of other theories. For example, some hold that the

writer was favorable to Galilean Christianity and, like Mark
and Matthew, wished to close the resurrection stories in Galilee rather than Judea (v. 1). If the epilogue was for that purpose, it certainly achieves much more. Others hold the view
that the epilogue is an addition from the Petrine circle, calling attention to the focus upon Peter in four of the five
paragraphs. In support, Luke 5:3–7 is cited, the Synoptic
parallel to the fishing story of vv. 4–8 in which Simon Peter
is prominent. In addition, Luke 24:34 and 1 Cor 15:5 refer to
a resurrection appearance to Simon. And finally, the shepherd imagery of vv. 15–19 is said to accord well with 1 Peter
5:1–5. But if this is a Petrine edition, why does the Beloved
Disciple remain in the epilogue the disciple closest to the
Lord? Other perspectives no more nor less persuasive have
been taken.

The preacher must not allow the number and inconclu-
sive nature of these positions to discourage the effort to find
a defensible and fruitful angle of vision upon these verses. In
fact, looking at the text from several positions can be most
enlightening and enable one to preach refreshingly from
within the circle of the Gospel's impact upon its early readers. And even when one comes short of a firm conclusion as
to the author's primary intent, rich insights flow from such
study which are not invalidated by uncertainty of intention.
These insights are sometimes called "the surplus of meaning" found in a biblical text. Consider a few lines of thought
fruitful for preaching which do no violence to the epilogue
nor to the whole Gospel.

The post-Easter decline common to almost every church
can trace its ancestry to the original disciples. What does the
church do after Easter: Peter said, "I am going fishing."
Christ is risen, hosanna! Christ has ascended, farewell. Meanwhile, back at the Church what happens next? Religious experiences as glorious as Easter leave us back where we were
unless Easter is followed by Pentecost and unless the believer's experience of Christ is translated into concrete assignments of discipleship. Churches that try to avoid the post-
Easter slump by trying for a "Super Sunday" the next week
are trapped in a self-defeating effort. Only so many rabbits
can come out of the hat. It would be better to study this
chapter. Simon Peter's return to the old life was treated with

assignments to particular tasks: feed and care for the sheep. There is more therapy, more health, more genuine Christianity in a job to be done than in adding to the number of balloons on the ceiling.

Or the preacher may choose to call attention to the liturgical nature of this chapter. Eating together as an occasion for experiencing the presence of Christ had established itself quite early in the practice and thinking of the early church (1 Cor 11:23–24; Luke 24:28–35). Luke says the risen Lord "was known to them in the breaking of bread" (24:35), and tells of Christ eating broiled fish with his disciples after the resurrection (24:41–42). The conversations and events of John 21 occur over a meal of fish and bread. If those scholars are right who say this and other passages in the Fourth Gospel grew out of and were used in Christian worship assemblies, then an important message could explore what really occurred when the Christian community gathered for worship. There was, according to our text, food shared and fellowship with each other. There was also the renewal of the believers' relationship with the risen Christ. According to vv. 12–14, it was also an occasion which confirmed and encouraged faith. But in addition, worship was a time when Christ confronted his followers and pressed them to answer anew the question, "Do you love Me?" (vv. 15–19). Faith's response was not to be in words alone but in action in all ways that love for Christ demonstrates itself in human caring (vv. 15–17). Finally, before departing the worshipers heard again the word of Christ that had first brought them to him and to each other, "Follow me" (v. 19). This is not a bad checklist for evaluating our own worship life as a church.

A third suggestion for developing John 21 into a message to the church is to concentrate upon Christ's words, "Follow me." The command just stands there alone, without details, without suggestions, without further instructions. In fact, the Fourth Gospel is famous for enjoining obedience, keeping Christ's word, following faithfully and obeying his commandments but without specifying exactly what that involves. Now here again, Christ says, "Follow me." Where? To do what? What does it mean to be a disciple of Jesus Christ? Perhaps some clue lies in the stories of Peter and the Beloved Disciple (vv. 18–23). For Simon Peter discipleship meant

martyrdom (vv. 18–19), and so it did, and does, for countless
thousands of others. But martyrdom was not the only form of
discipleship, as Peter was to learn when he sought to turn
attention from himself to the Beloved Disciple (vv. 20–21).
Jesus' word to Peter was clear: the nature of your discipleship is not to be confused with that of any other. The other
disciple may be called upon to take another path, but that is
not your concern. Christians are not to compare and contrast
themselves with each other as though they were being grad-
ed on the curve. Whoever takes the path of discipleship cannot know where it will lead. The disciple can only know that
at the end of it is Christ.

Bibliography

Preparation for preaching on the Gospel of John involves working in at least two kinds of books: commentaries and studies in Johannine theology.

As to commentaries, two are strongly urged:

Raymond E. Brown, *The Gospel According to John*. The Anchor Bible. 2 vols. (Garden City, N.Y: Doubleday, 1966, 1970). Offers a fresh translation, detailed notes on every verse, and solid interpretation of the text.

Rudolf Bultmann, *The Gospel of John: A Commentary*, tr. G. R. Beasley-Murray *et al.* (Philadelphia: Westminster, 1971). First appeared in German in 1941 and every major work on John since that time has had to converse with this stimulating study.

Theological reflections on the Gospel are essential for an overview and for coming to clarity on major issues. Three such studies are recommended:

D. M. Smith, *John*. Proclamation Commentaries (Philadelphia, Fortress, 1976). A clear, concise and balanced view of the theology of John.

E. Käsemann, *The Testament of Jesus*, tr. G. Krodel (Philadelphia: Fortress, 1968). Places John near the edge of Gnostic heresy, contra the view of Brown.

Robert Kysar, *John, the Maverick Gospel* (Atlanta: John Knox Press, 1976). Written for the beginning student, but by a writer thoroughly familiar with John. Fresh and germinal.

For the preacher who wishes to explore how the Gospel of John was understood in the church for which it was written, a thoughtful (at times speculative) study has been written by Raymond Brown, *The Community of the Beloved Disciple* (New York: Paulist Press, 1979).

For a review of modern interpretations of this Gospel, see Robert Kysar, *The Fourth Evangelist and His Gospel* (Minneapolis: Augsburg, 1975). A bit demanding, but well organized and thorough.